THE EVOLUTION OF SINGLE LIFE TO LIFE PARTNERSHIP

Discover Clinical Practice Techniques to Maintain the
Spark or Rekindle Flames

KATHERINE IBARRA

Contents

This book is dedicated to the loving memory of both my mom, Jeanelle Stovall and my Godmother, Katherine Dunham. Both of these incredible women ingrained in me the teachings of self-love, compassion and humility. I also want to dedicate this book to my ever-loving and supportive husband, Nathan and to my two beautiful daughters, Isabella and Celeste who are my biggest fans and who inspire me everyday to keep reaching for the stars.

Introduction

When you're rushing in the mornings to get yourself ready, get the kids ready for school, and go to work, do you do a quick peck on the cheek of your spouse and say "bye!" or do you take a moment to kiss your spouse on the lips for at least 6 seconds and say "I love you, have a good day!"? Dr. John Ottman, a marriage and family therapist, and his wife, Dr. Julie Schwartz Gottman, a clinical psychologist, coined the term 6-second kiss rule. They determined after a study of 70,000 people in 24 countries that couples kissing each other for at least 6 seconds secrete oxytocin, contributing to a consistent sense of psychological safety and long-term happiness and success.

I am Katherine Ibarra, a licensed clinical psychotherapist with over 16 years of experience in adult mental health. I am also the author of "5 Categories of Self Care: The Ultimate Guide to Finding Self Love and Happiness." Throughout my career, I have dedicated myself to understanding the intricacies of human relationships. My passion for this field stems from a deep-seated belief in the transformative power of love and commitment, coupled with effective communication and mutual respect. This book is a culmination of years spent working with patients, helping patients and their partners navigate the complexities of their relationships to build a foundation of lasting love and respect.

"The Evolution of Single Life to Life Partnership" offers practical tools, exercises, and insights to enhance communication, deepen emotional and physical intimacy, and improve relationship health. This book stands apart for its blend of clinical techniques with engaging, interactive content that you can apply directly in your daily interactions with your partner.

In the following chapters, we will explore critical themes essential for any thriving relationship: effective communication strategies, trust building and rebuilding, conflict management, enhancing emotional and physical intimacy, personal growth, and coping with external pressures. Each section includes practical exercises and techniques grounded in clinical practice and research, ensuring their relevance and efficacy. We will also assess and detect unhealthy traits of a partnership that may be toxic and explore if the partnership is sustainable in the long term.

As adults committed to enhancing their relationships, whether navigating specific challenges or simply aiming to deepen their connection, this book acknowledges the diversity of their experiences and life stages. It offers valuable insights that are applicable across a spectrum of scenarios.

Approaching this guide with an open mind to clinical techniques will unlock transformative potential in your relationship and personal growth. This book is crafted to be accessible, engaging, and devoid of jargon, making complex psychological concepts understandable and relatable. The tone is warm, encouraging, and supportive, inviting you on a journey of discovery and growth.

Please engage actively with the content, apply the exercises, reflect on your progress, and embrace the path to a healthier, more fulfilling relationship. This journey begins with the steps you are about to take, and I am here to guide you through each one.

As we embark on this path together, remember that the capacity for change and growth within yourself and your relationship is immense. My commitment to your journey is unwavering, and I hope this book serves as a valuable guide and companion. Let's begin this transformative adventure with the ultimate goal of deeper connections and a renewed sense of partnership.

Welcome to "The Evolution of Single Life to Life Partnership" Let's start this meaningful journey together.

ONE

Assessing if a Relationship Is Co-dependent and Toxic

Have you ever wondered if what you're feeling in your relationship is what they call "love" or if it's something a bit less healthy? You're not alone in this. Many people find themselves in relationships that don't just rock the boat but threaten to sink it. Understanding whether your relationship is co-dependent or toxic is the crucial first step towards transforming it into a healthier, happier partnership.

Gas Lighting Warning Signs and Narcissism

Let's talk about a sneaky culprit often lurking in the shadows of troubled relationships: narcissism. Recognizing the signs is like finally finding glasses with the correct prescription – things make much more sense. Narcissists often weave a web of manipulation that can make you question your sanity. One of their favorite tricks? Gaslighting. This is where Gaslighters manipulate you into questioning your memory, perception, or sanity. Say you saw them flirting at a party; they'll twist it around and have you apologizing by the end of the conversation for being 'too sensitive' or 'misinterpreting' things.

Wondering if you're dealing with a narcissist? Look out for these red flags: a grandiose sense of self-importance, fantasies about unlimited success or beauty, a belief that they're special and unique and can only be understood by, or should associate with, other special or high-status people, a need for excessive admiration, a sense of entitlement, interpersonally exploitative behavior, a lack of empathy, envy of others or a belief that others are envious of them, and demonstration of arrogant and haughty behaviors or attitudes.

Let's review common gas lighting warning signs and see if any resonate with your relationship.

1. The gaslighter denies that an event or something they said ever happened, and you question your memory. Gaslighter: "I never said that! You're remembering wrong!"
2. The gaslighter will often minimize your concern and be condescending or dismissive. Gaslighter: "You're making a big deal out of nothing."
3. The gaslighter will lie to your face even if you have evidence of deceit, and you still wonder, "Maybe I am being overcritical?"
4. Over time, the gaslighter will destroy your sense of safety in a relationship—not only that sense of physical safety but also emotional safety, the ability to express your feelings and intellectually express your thoughts without fear of retaliation.
5. The gaslighter will project the very wrongdoing they are guilty of onto you. "Maybe you're the one who is lying! Or maybe you're the one who is cheating."

But let's remember the green flags that signal a healthy relationship: open communication, mutual respect, trust, support, and a genuine partnership where you both celebrate each other's successes. Recognizing these can reassure you that you're on the right track.

Let's review common Green Flags and see if any of these signs resonate in your relationship. Hopefully, most of these signs will.

1. You are each independently happy together and also time apart through friendships or different interests and hobbies.
2. You appreciate one another, support each other, and often express gratitude.
3. You are committed to the relationship equally and invest time and energy towards that relationship.
4. You are both able to communicate effectively using assertive communication. In assertive communication, you respect yourself and the other person, clearly state your needs and wants, and provide compromise—or solution-focused ideas.
5. You both show empathy and attempt to understand each other's points of view, even if you don't necessarily agree.
6. You are both transparent and honest with one another. Actions speak louder than words, so what you say needs to match your actions consistently.
7. You must share specific goals, beliefs, and values; however, it is also important to have interests and goals different from your partner's.

8. In relationships, it is essential that you not only feel close physically but also have that emotional connection.

9. All green flags are equally important; however, the green flag of safety is incredibly crucial in maintaining stability and trust in a relationship. You should feel safe physically of course, but also emotionally, be able to express feelings and intellectually, be able to express thoughts without feeling that you have to walk on eggshells.

10. You should not feel you must present a particular facade in a relationship to be accepted. You should be your true, authentic self and proud.

Self-care is your secret weapon in dealing with and healing from toxic relationships. Remember the 5 Categories of Self Care referenced in my previous guidebook. Think of self-care in five categories: Physical (getting enough sleep and exercise), emotional (talking about problems with a friend/therapist or journaling), social (spending time with friends who lift you up), spiritual (meditation or spending time in nature and reflecting on what is meaningful to you), and professional (pursuing your career goals and advocating for self). Engaging in these forms of self-care can empower you, boost your self-esteem, and strengthen your emotional independence, which is crucial when considering stepping away from a toxic relationship. I encourage you to delve deeper with my guidebook, "5 Categories of Self Care: The Ultimate Guide to Finding Self-Love and Happiness".

Navigating away from toxicity and towards healthier relationships isn't just about leaving; it's about transforming your mindset and building the inner strength necessary to recognize and demand the love and respect you deserve. Just like building muscle, it takes consistent effort and the right tools, but it is worth it when you see the results.

In personal disclosure, I was in a toxic relationship and was gaslit often without even realizing it. Many around me had no idea because they always considered me as a strong and independent woman. I was a shell of myself though and doubted myself and my opinions often. I always apologized, and many times, I had no idea why. It was a defense mechanism to appease and avoid potential adverse reactions or anger outbursts. I finally was able to acknowledge after seven years that I was not in a healthy relationship and ultimately did not feel that complete sense of safety.

I left that relationship, did some soul-searching, and worked on the five categories of self-care. I regained a sense of self and self-esteem and became independently happy. At that time, I had reached independent happiness and met my now husband, Nathan, who also had reached his independent happiness. We complimented each other's strengths, and we elevated each other's happiness on the daily. We vowed to continue elevating each other's happiness for the rest of our lives. So far, so good. We had our 10th wedding anniversary in July 2024.

TWO

The Essence of Communication in Relationships

Have you ever felt like you and your partner spoke different languages? It's like that episode from your favorite sitcom where the couple misinterprets each other's words and spirals into a comical yet distressing misunderstanding. Much of what we "say" isn't about the words at all. Non-verbal communication—our gestures, facial expressions, and tone—plays a starring role in how we communicate with our partners. This chapter dives into the silent symphony of non-verbal communication that underscores every interaction with your significant other, often saying more than words could ever convey.

Understanding Communication Barriers

Ever found yourself nodding along during a conversation only to realize later that you have absolutely no clue what was agreed upon? That's passive hearing in a nutshell. It's like when you autopilot through your morning routine and can't remember if you shampooed your hair twice. On the other hand, active listening is about fully engaging with your partner, soaking in every word, and responding thoughtfully. It's the difference between just hearing the music and moving rhythmically to its beat. Active listening involves understanding the content, the emotions behind it, and responding in a way that builds further conversation, rather than just waiting for your turn to speak.

We will next assess your communication skills by reviewing what Dr. John Gottman famously dubbed the "Four Horsemen and Antidotes."

The **four horsemen** are harmful behaviors that become a normal way of communicating but slowly eat away at the fabric of a strong relationship over time.

Antidotes are skills and different ways of thinking to replace each of the four horsemen and create a space for a more positive connection with each other.

The Four Horsemen and Antidotes

Horsemen # 1 Criticism: Very critical of the person and flaws rather than focusing more on changeable behaviors. You tend to be very hostile and defensive.

Example: "You forgot to take out the trash! You never get anything done around the house!"

Antidote #1: Gentle Startup: Approach the conversation in a gentle and respectful way. Be mindful that your body language and tone of voice are warm and inviting. Keep it on the "I."

Example: "I feel frustrated at times, because I feel like there is an uneven share of household duties. I am wondering if we could talk about how we could make it more even?"

Horsemen #2 Defensiveness: A person deflects responsibilities for their own behaviors and actions, and refuses to take any feedback without taking it personally. Often shifts blame back on partner and projects their own flaws.

Example: "It isn't my fault that I got upset with you, you don't listen to what I am saying."

Antidote #2: Take Accountability: Own up to your own behaviors without blaming anyone else, and apologize when appropriate.

Example: "I am sorry I raised my voice at you. I will try to work on not raising my voice and being more assertive in communication instead of being aggressive in my communication."

Horsemen #3 Contempt: Having built up anger, resentment, disgust, and hostility towards partner.

Example: "You're such an idiot for forgetting our anniversary!"

Antidote #1: Share Fondness & Gratitude: You approach the conversation lovingly. Think about your partner's strengths, and give compliments when appropriate.

Example: "You usually are the one that is romantic, and remember every single date. That's what I love about you. I guess I was hurt that you seemed to have forgotten this year. Can we talk about ways that we can have a make-up anniversary outing?"

Horsemen #4 Stonewalling: A person shuts down all communication due to feeling overwhelmed. It is a defense mechanism and often that individual retreats physically or says nothing.The problem continues to go unresolved though, and the other person becomes more frustrated and holds resentment.

Antidote #1 Breath: You want to use relaxation techniques. Be mindful of your physical symptoms when you are starting to get upset. Is your heart racing, hands shaking, voice quivering? If yes, verbalize "I am feeling overwhelmed right now. I need to take a little walk, but I do want to come back to this conversation after both of us have calmed down and we can talk about compromises and solution focused ideas in order to have a more productive conversation."

Now, let's add another layer: the spectrum of communication. It's not just about the words you choose; it's how you say them. Your tone, your body language, and even your facial expressions pack a punch in delivering your message. You could say "fine" in a way that means anything from genuinely okay to 'I'm quite upset.' Misinterpretations can arise from these non-verbal cues, too. For instance, a crossed arm might be considered defensive when you're cold! These small cues require attention, as they are often louder than words.

Cultural differences add another twist to this complex dance. In some cultures, direct eye contact is seen as confidence; in others, it's perceived as disrespect. Understanding these nuances is crucial. It's like knowing the basic steps of a dance in different styles – without them, you're bound to step on some toes. Enhancing your observation skills to pick up on these subtle non-verbal cues will make you a better dancer in the rhythm of your relationship. Pay attention to your partner's gestures, facial expressions, and even the changes in their tone. It's about noticing the small things that say a lot.

And, let's not forget about the love languages – words of affirmation, acts of service, receiving gifts, quality time, and physical touch. Understanding your and your partner's primary love language can transform how you perceive and deliver love. It's like knowing exactly which ingredients your partner loves in a dish – it turns a good meal into their comfort food. For example, if your partner cherishes quality time more than anything, they might appreciate a weekend getaway more than a fancy gift. Recognizing and speaking each other's love languages fluently can significantly reduce misunderstandings and deepen your connection.

Navigating through these communication barriers requires patience and a lot of practice. But with a bit of humor, a lot of love, and an understanding of these principles, you'll master the art of conversation in no time, turning misunderstandings into opportunities for growth and connection.

The Role of Active Listening in Preventing Misunderstandings

Let's face it: misunderstandings can turn a perfect day into a soap opera episode faster than you can say, "What did you mean by that?" That's where the superpower of active listening comes in. It's more than just nodding while your partner talks; it's about truly understanding what they're saying, feeling, and needing. Think of it as the difference between hearing the lyrics of a song and feeling its rhythm pulse through you.

Now, empathy is the heart of active listening. It's what allows you not just to hear but deeply understand your partner's words and emotions. Imagine you're talking about how stressed you are at work, and instead of getting solutions thrown at you, your partner says, "That sounds tough; tell me more about what's making it so hard?" That's empathy. It's about acknowledging your feelings and diving into them with you. Empathy builds bridges; it connects your emotional islands and lets you know you're not alone.

However, empathy shouldn't be confused with sympathy. Empathy sits with you during your grief, while sympathy sends flowers after the funeral. Sympathy might say, "I'm sorry you're feeling this way," whereas empathy says, "I'm here with you in this feeling." See the difference? Sympathy is observed from a distance; empathy shares the experience up close. This distinction is crucial in relationships because feeling understood on a deep, emotional level can turn a brewing storm into a passing cloud.

Building empathy isn't just a nice-to-have; it's a must-have, and like any skill, it takes practice. Try this: practice reflective listening the next time your partner shares something important. This means mirroring back what you heard them say. For example, if your partner is upset about a friend canceling plans, you might reflect, "It sounds like you're hurt because you were looking forward to spending time with them." This shows you're paying attention and helps your partner feel genuinely heard and understood.

But let's not sugarcoat it—there are natural barriers to active listening. Distractions are everywhere. From buzzing phones to buzzing thoughts about your to-do list, it's easy to be only half-present. Emotional reactions can also hijack your listening skills. If something your partner says triggers you, you might miss what comes next because you're too busy formulating your defense. And let's not forget about preconceptions; if you've already decided what your partner means before they even finish speaking, you're not listening, are you?

Improving your active listening skills can be a game-changer. Start with the basics: maintain eye contact, nod to show you're engaged, and resist the urge to interrupt. Then, level up by paraphrasing your partner's words and asking open-ended questions to delve deeper. For instance, instead of "You're such a stickler with money and always saying no to everything!" Maybe try saying something like, "I hear you. You are feeling worried about money right now and that we need to limit the number of vacations, at least for this year?"

Three Forms of Communication to keep in mind

Remember the three forms of communication referenced in my guidebook "5 Categories of Self Care: The Ultimate Guide to Finding Self Love and Happiness"? Let's recap: We will review three common forms of communication, and I need you to identify and acknowledge the type of communication style you use in different settings, including significant others, family, friends, and work/supervisors/co-workers.

Passive Communicator: Do you often stay quiet to avoid conflict and find yourself always prioritizing other people's feelings and needs over your own? This type of communicator tends to neglect their own wants and needs and as a result, even well-meaning individuals may unintentionally take advantage of them due to the passive communicator's failure to communicate effectively

Common traits for passive communicators include:

- Soft spoken
- Allows others to take advantage
- Prioritizes needs of others
- Makes poor eye contact
- Does not express wants/needs
- Lacks confidence

Aggressive Communicator: An individual may prioritize only their own needs, wants, and feelings while disregarding those of others.

Common traits for Aggressive communicators include:

- Easily Frustrated
- Speaks in a loud or overbearing way
- Unwilling to compromise
- Use of criticism, humiliation and domination
- Frequently interrupts or does not listen
- Disrespectful towards others

Assertive Communicator: This communication style is effective in any situation, whether with family, friends, coworkers, or significant others. Assertive communication emphasizes the importance of addressing the needs of both parties. An assertive communicator respects themselves and the other party, and can clearly state their needs, wants, and feelings, as well as listen to and respect the needs of others. Assertive communicators are confident and willing to find compromises or offer solution-focused ideas.

Common traits for Assertive communicators include:

- Listens without interruption
- Clearly states needs and wants
- Makes good eye contact
- Willing to compromise
- Stands up for self
- Confident tone/body language

Example Scenario using all three types of communication:

Scenario: You are working from home remotely and are swamped. You go to the kitchen to grab a quick snack and notice a complete mess that your partner left in the kitchen. Meanwhile, your partner is off work and binge-watching the show Valhalla on the living room couch.

Passive Response: You don't say anything, so just go ahead and clean the mess even though you don't have the time. (Your internal monologue says, "I am sick of this constantly happening!! I always have to clean up around my slob of a partner!")

Aggressive Response: "You're such a slob. Can you clean up the mess in the kitchen?"

Assertive Response: "Hey babe, I am swamped now with work. It would be super helpful if you could clear up the kitchen now so that when I am wrapping up work, I can go straight to prepping for dinner and not worry about cleaning first?"

Do you see how the assertive communicator respects self and partner, states needs and wants, and presents compromise? That assertive communicator clearly states their wants and needs for help in this situation and provides solution-focused ideas and compromise that could resolve the problem and prevent it from becoming a major blowup.

Assertive communication is crucial in every setting. Remember that assertive communication is not aggressive communication. Being assertive means remaining calm, respecting both yourself and the other person, and providing solution-focused ideas that make both parties feel like active participants in working towards more positive outcomes and preventing a recurring negative outcome.

Reflective Listening Exercise Tips

Active listening isn't just about hearing words; it's about fully engaging with your partner's feelings, words, and, most importantly, their heart. It creates a foundation of trust and understanding critical for nurturing love and empathy. When you listen actively, you're not just waiting for your turn to speak; you're truly present, soaking in every word with the intent to understand, not to respond. This level of attentiveness tells your partner, "I value you, and what you have to say matters to me."

Try this simple exercise tonight: When conversing with your partner, consciously adjust your body language to reflect openness and attentiveness. Uncross your arms, lean in slightly, and nod to show you're engaged. After the conversation, reflect on how this small change impacted the interaction. Did it invite more openness? How did your partner respond? This awareness can be a powerful tool in strengthening your connection.

Improving your active listening skills can seem daunting, but it's manageable with some straightforward techniques. Mirroring and summarizing are particularly effective. Mirroring involves repeating back what your partner has said, not parrot-style, but in your own words. For instance, if your partner is upset about having a rough day at work, you might respond, "It sounds like you had a challenging day, and it's been quite tough on you." This shows you're paying attention and helps clarify that you've understood their message correctly. Summarizing, conversely, is about wrapping up the key points of a more extended dialogue, which can be especially helpful in more complex or emotionally charged discussions.

By mastering the subtle art of non-verbal communication, you and your partner can enhance your understanding of each other, paving the way for deeper, more meaningful interactions. Remember, in the dance of communication, every gesture, every look, every tone speaks volumes. So, tune into this silent language and watch how it transforms your relationship, one unspoken word at a time.

Active listening also plays a pivotal role in resolving conflicts. Picture this scenario: you're arguing, voices are raised, and emotions are flaring. Now, what if, in that moment, you chose to listen to what's driving your partner's frustration instead of adding fuel to the fire? Active listening can help de-escalate conflicts by making both parties feel heard and understood. It's not about agreeing with each other all the time but about acknowledging each other's feelings and perspectives. When both partners feel that their voices are heard, finding a middle ground and working through disagreements with compassion and respect becomes easier.

Embracing these active listening practices can transform how you communicate with your partner. It turns everyday conversations into opportunities for deeper connection and understanding, paving the way for a relationship is not just about coexisting but genuinely thriving together. As you continue to hone these skills, you'll likely notice a shift in how you relate to your partner and how responsive and open they become in return. It's a beautiful cycle of mutual respect and understanding that strengthens your bond significantly.

Navigating Difficult Conversations with Compassion

Think of the last time you had to bring up something touchy with your partner. It could be about finances, in-laws, potential in-laws, or perhaps even your feelings about the relationship. Your heart was probably racing, and your palms may have been a bit sweaty. It's like standing at the edge of a diving board over a chilly pool, knowing you need to jump but not wanting to. This is where approaching sensitive topics with compassion sets the stage for a more positive outcome, transforming what could be a cold plunge into a more gentle entry.

Starting with compassion means choosing your words with care and being attuned to the emotional temperature of the conversation. It's about ensuring your partner feels safe and understood, not on trial. An effective way to do this is using "I" statements instead of the accusatory "you" phrases. For example, saying, "I feel worried when we don't talk about our budget," instead of "You never discuss finances with me!" This minor linguistic tweak can make a difference, reducing defensiveness and opening up a space for more honest and productive communication.

Timing, they say, is everything, and this couldn't be truer than when it comes to difficult conversations. Imagine bringing up your frustration with your partner's spending habits as they're stressed about an upcoming work deadline. Chances are, that conversation will end poorly. Choosing the right moment is considering your partner's current state and environment. Sometimes, it's worth waiting for a calm evening at home, perhaps after a meal when you're more relaxed and receptive. It's not about avoiding the conversation but respecting the timing to ensure it can be as constructive as possible.

Maintaining your cool in the heat of a stern talk is like trying to stay dry under a waterfall—it's tricky but not impossible. The key lies in managing your own emotions first. Techniques like deep breathing, pausing before responding, and actively reminding yourself of the conversation's goal can help maintain calm. Remember, the aim is not to 'win' the argument but to understand each other better and find a solution that works for both of you. If you feel the conversation is starting to escalate, it's okay to suggest a short break. A five-minute walk or even stepping into another room to collect your thoughts can prevent the discussion from becoming a battleground.

Finally, how you move forward after a difficult conversation can define the future trajectory of your relationship. It's like navigating a ship after a storm; repairs might be necessary, but you're both committed to reaching the shore together. A constructive follow-up might involve outlining what was agreed upon, discussing any compromises made, and expressing gratitude for each other's willingness to work through the issue. It's also helpful to plan check-ins to revisit the topic and see how the solutions are progressing. This reinforces the resolutions and deepens trust, showing that you both take your commitments seriously.

Remember, the goal of communication in a relationship isn't to avoid conflict altogether but to handle it so that both partners feel heard, respected, and loved. By approaching sensitive topics with care, choosing the right moments for discussions, managing your emotions effectively, and thoughtfully moving forward after tough conversations, you're not just solving problems. You're deepening your connection, enhancing your understanding, and fortifying your partnership against future storms. With these strategies, even the most challenging conversations can become opportunities for growth and increased intimacy.

THREE

The Role of Trust and Vulnerability

S omething that often gets a bad rap in our tough-it-out culture is vulnerability. It's like that old, creaky door in your house that you might not want to open because who knows what's behind it? Dusty skeletons? A forgotten treasure? Opening up can feel a bit like that; it's a gamble. But here's the twist: embracing vulnerability isn't just about airing out the skeletons; it's also about discovering the treasures of deeper intimacy in your relationship. Showing vulnerability is also a beautiful tool for apologizing and taking accountability because it shows that you care for the other person and want them to feel better and heard.

Cultivating Vulnerability: The Strength in Being Open

So, why do we often view vulnerability as a weakness? It could be old-school playground rules taught us to keep our guard up. Or perhaps it's Hollywood, with its rugged, stoic heroes who never seem to shed a tear. But here's the reality: vulnerability is a superpower in relationships. The secret sauce can transform your relationship to extraordinary levels of deeper connection. When you open up about your fears, dreams, and insecurities, you're not just sharing information but inviting your partner into your inner world. This isn't just about being open; it's about being open-hearted, and that's where true intimacy starts to bloom.

Now, how do you create a safe space for this kind of openness? Cultivating a safe space for vulnerability means making sure there's warmth and understanding, where judgment is suspended, and where there is a sense of welcome. Each time you receive a supportive response, it reinforces the safety of sharing, gradually deepening the trust between you and your partner.

Speaking of trust, the sturdy frame supports the whole house of vulnerability. When you share a vulnerable truth, and your partner meets you with empathy, it's like adding a brick to the foundation of your trust. This mutual exchange does wonders for your relationship's trust bank. Think of it like this: whenever you're open with your partner, and they respond with care, you're both saying, "I trust you with my heart." And as this trust grows, so does your connection, creating a virtuous cycle of openness and intimacy.

But let's address the elephant in the room—fear. Opening up can be downright scary. What if your partner laughs at your dreams? Or worse, what if they dismiss you or belittle you? These worries are the guardians of your vulnerability, and they don't let down their guard easily. To overcome these fears, start with something small, something that feels risky but not terrifying. Share that strange dream you had last night or why a particular date on the calendar is significant to you. It's like testing the waters before a swim. As you experience more positive interactions, your confidence will grow, making it easier to share more profound, more personal aspects of yourself.

Journaling Prompt: Exploring Your Vulnerability

Grab a journal and consider this prompt: Write about a time you were vulnerable, which led to a positive outcome in your relationship. How did it feel? What did it change between you and your partner? Reflecting on these moments can build your confidence in the power of openness.

By embracing vulnerability, you're not just opening that creaky old door; you're letting in the light, clearing out the cobwebs, and uncovering treasures that deepen and enrich your relationship in ways you never imagined. So, let down those guards a little, open that door, and see what wonders await on the other side of vulnerability.

The Art of an Apology

Remember the earlier discussion on the 4 Horsemen and Antidotes? One of the Horsemen is Defensiveness; you deflect and blame everyone else, and you have difficulty not taking feedback personally. Instead, attempt to practice the antidote of showing vulnerability, empathy, and warmth as you take accountability for your actions and apologize for your part in a situation that hurt or upset the other party. Using these antidotes will help repair a damaged relationship and show deep respect and love for one another.

3 Simple Steps in Apologizing:

Step 1 Self-Reflection: Reflect on yourself in a given situation. How did my actions contribute to the problem? As best as you can, try to see the situation from the other person's perspective and understand why they may be upset.

Step 2: Accountability: Even if the other person contributed to the problem, you need to be accountable for your actions. "I see why you were upset that I laughed at what you shared as your dream goal. It was insensitive, and I apologize for that."

Step 3: Listen and Learn: Remember reflective listening? Listen to the other person, and do not interrupt. Forgiveness can take time, but showing warmth, empathy, and that you're listening is a great start in starting a productive conversation about how to prevent the situation from repeating and ways to help rebuild that trust and love for each other.

True and False Statements

False: "I never have to say 'I'm sorry' in a relationship because my partner already knows."

True: Apologizing is vital in showing that you care and love your partner deeply, want to ensure they feel better, and want to make sure that the same situation will not repeat itself.

False: "I said I was sorry. That should be enough."

True: Remember that all three steps need to be incorporated into a genuine apology in order for it to really hold substance and productivity.

False: "Apologizing means I let the other person win the argument."

True: A true apology shows that you respect yourself and the other party, and are willing to acknowledge your contribution to the problem, and want to work to resolve it because you deeply care for one another.

Imagine empathy as the secret antidote in apologies that helps cure and heal a damaged relationship. At its core, empathy involves stepping into your partner's shoes, feeling what they feel, and seeing the world through their eyes. It's not just about understanding their joy and pain from your perspective but genuinely experiencing it as if it were your own. When you practice empathy, you're not just near your partner; you're there with them, right in the emotional thick of it. This shared emotional experience can knit you closer together, weaving a fabric of intimacy that's tough to tear.

Developing empathic communication can be very natural for some individuals, and for others, it takes a lot of practice. For those individuals for whom it does not come naturally, be patient, be intentional, and with hard work, it can become fluid and feel almost effortless. One critical step is reflective listening. This isn't just about hearing words; it's about listening with the intent to understand and reflect what your partner is feeling.

Another game changer in empathic communication is validation. Validation doesn't mean you agree with everything your partner says or feels; it's about acknowledging their feelings as valid and understandable. If your partner is anxious about an upcoming family gathering, instead of brushing off their feelings with a "It'll be fine," you might say, "It makes sense you're feeling anxious, given how tense things have been.

How can I support you?" This kind of response validates their feelings and opens up a space for support and cooperation rather than dismissal and isolation.

Empathy also plays a starring role in resolving conflicts. Imagine you're both upset because plans keep getting postponed. Instead of harboring resentment, try to empathize with each other's feelings. Perhaps your partner is disappointed because they were looking forward to those plans, while you might feel pressured and overwhelmed by scheduling conflicts. By sharing and understanding these feelings, you can turn a potential conflict into a moment of mutual understanding and problem-solving.

With empathy at times, we all encounter barriers—stress, exhaustion, personal biases, or simply the complexities of our own emotions. These barriers can make it challenging to maintain an empathetic stance. Recognizing these obstacles is the first step in navigating through them. When stressed or overwhelmed, it's easy to become wrapped up in our feelings and needs, making it harder to attend to our partner's emotions. Acknowledging this can help you take a step back, breathe, and approach the situation with renewed focus and empathy. Additionally, challenging your biases and preconceptions can open up new ways of understanding and relating to your partner, deepening your emotional connection.

As we wrap up this chapter on emotional intimacy, we've explored the importance of daily rituals, sharing your deepest selves, and the transformative power of empathy. These elements deepen your connection with your partner, creating a rich understanding, support, and loving relationship. In the next chapter, we'll focus on healing after betrayal and moving towards forgiveness and explore possible ways to reignite that physical intimacy and emotional closeness.

Healing After Betrayal: Steps Toward Forgiveness

Betrayal in a relationship can feel like a rug has been pulled out from under you, and suddenly, everything you trust is up in the air. It's messy, it's painful, and yes, it's downright disorienting. Healing from such a deep wound is not a linear process; it's more like navigating a labyrinth where you encounter a range of emotions, from disbelief and anger to sadness and, eventually, acceptance. Embracing this process with patience and self-compassion is crucial. It's okay to feel hurt, and it's OK to take time to grieve the broken trust. This isn't about rushing to "get over" the betrayal but allowing yourself the space to understand and heal at your own pace fully.

During this time, nurturing self-compassion is like applying a soothing balm to a burn. It can be tempting to blame yourself or dwell on "what-ifs" and "if-only." Instead, gently remind yourself that you're doing your best under challenging circumstances. Healing is about permitting yourself to feel whatever comes up without judgment. Think of it as your best friend, offering comfort and understanding to yourself when you need it most. This kind of self-care sets a solid foundation for genuine healing and forgiveness.

Forgiveness, often misunderstood, is usually seen as a quick fix. However, true forgiveness in the context of betrayal is a powerful act of emotional bravery; it does not mean condoning the hurtful actions or wiping the slate clean without accountability. Instead, forgiveness is about freeing yourself from the burden of bitterness. It allows you to move forward without carrying the weight of past hurts. To start, reframing forgiveness as a gift to yourself rather than to the person who wronged you can be helpful. This shift in perspective can be incredibly freeing and pave the way for rebuilding trust if you choose to continue the relationship.

Rebuilding trust is the most intricate part of healing from betrayal. It requires consistent effort and transparency from both partners. For the betrayer, this means being an open book. From sharing passwords to keeping promises, every gesture is just an attempt to rebuild the bridge of trust. For the betrayed, it involves the gradual willingness to trust again, recognizing that this process is often two steps forward, one step back. It's not about immediate forgiveness or a return to how things were but a slow rebuilding of trust through consistent and honest behavior. Regular check-ins can also be a practical way to foster transparency. These include weekly discussions about feelings and the healing process, which can reinforce the commitment to recovery.

Forgiveness Therapy

Forgiveness Therapy is one of my most favorite tools in helping my patients process and heal in a healthier and more productive way. Forgiveness Therapy based on a model by Dr. Robert D. Enright, can be utilized in any setting whether it is discord with friends, coworkers, family members or your significant other. Many times patients initial reaction is "I am too angry to forgive!" or "(blank name) doesn't deserve forgiveness!" or "I hope (blank name) dies a painful death."

Try suspending pre-conceived notions of Forgiveness, and walk with me in changing your mindset on the true definition of Forgiveness and how it can help deepen your understanding of self and let go of the negative emotions connected to that person or event.

Remember that forgiveness is the decision to allow the pain from the past to no longer dictate your present and future. Forgiveness should be utilized for your personal growth and healing. It has nothing to do with the other person or their processing. It is about acknowledging the negative emotions (Anger, pain, shame, etc) associated with the person/event and letting go of the negative emotions. Harboring negative feelings only hurts you, preventing the process of healing and moving forward.

While Forgiveness is not about the other person, it is about attempting to gain additional perspectives on the other person/event. By gaining additional perspectives and insights, we can allow some space for compassion even though the other party is not entitled to it.

Now, what Forgiveness isn't? It is not about saying "I forgive you" and repairing a relationship. It is not about putting everything under the rug and forgetting what happened. It is not about making excuses or condoning behavior. It is not about granting legal mercy, and it is not about "letting go," but wishing revenge.

We will now review the four Phases of Forgiveness, which will provide a guide for navigating your Forgiveness Therapy journey.

1. **The Uncovering Phase**: This is where you really reflect on what happened, what were the injustices and how you have been impacted both emotionally and physically.

2. **The Decision Phase**: This where you really grasp the concept of what Forgiveness is, and if you choose to accept or reject Forgiveness as an option.

3. **The Work Phase**: This tends to be the more challenging phases as this is where you need to suspend judgment, and gain additional insight and perspective of the other person/event. Remember this is not making excuses for their behavior, but it is about trying to understand their learned behaviors and understand what they may have been thinking at the time of offense(s).

4. **The Deepening Phase**: Final phase! This is where hopefully you have been able to gain additional perspectives, and as a result have decreased negative emotions associated with what happened. You may even be able to identify silver linings, certain meanings in experiences and recognize self-growth.

Journal Prompts for Forgiveness Therapy

Keeping in mind #1 Uncovering Phase: Describe in a journal what happened. Why was this treatment unfair, unjust? How were you impacted? Painful emotions? Changed behaviors in other relationships? Practical costs, time, money? Have you changed outlook on life? Ie, "Trust no one, all people are evil." Do you experience cognitive rehearsal, recurring thoughts of what happened? And lastly did you experience any physical injuries from any abuse?

Keeping in mind #2 Decision Phase: Without looking at the definition of Forgiveness, I want you to write down how you would normally describe Forgiveness. Whether you have made the decision to use Forgiveness Therapy as an option, I want you to write down Pros and Cons of being able to let go of negative emotions associated with what happened.Think about how things for you might be different when you are not tied to these chains of hate, anger, resentment.

Keeping in mind #3 Work Phase: Remember this is to help gain perspective and insight. As best as you can answer the following questions. What was childhood, family dynamics like for the person who wronged you? Were there possible learned behaviors at that point? May this have played a role in certain behaviors in adulthood? What was going on at time of offense for the offender? In reflecting, were you able to gain some additional perspectives, which allowed room to lesson negative feelings?

Keeping in mind #4 Deepening Phase: Honestly answer self. Do you feel that you have benefitted from letting go of negative emotions, gaining insight and additional perspectives? Has Forgiveness Therapy helped you in finding new meanings in experiences, and recognizing your strengths and growth as a person?

There comes a point in healing where you might feel stuck or overwhelmed by emotions. This is a common juncture at which seeking professional help can be beneficial. Therapy isn't just for moments of crisis; it's a proactive tool for understanding and navigating your emotions and a space to learn how to rebuild the relationship with a stronger, more informed foundation. Whether it's individual counseling to sort through your feelings and understand yourself more or couples therapy to rebuild the relationship, professional guidance can provide the tools and perspective needed to navigate this challenging time effectively.

Try your best to remember that forgiveness is powerful and helps you move forward in life with or without your partner. It helps rebuild your sense of self and who you are individually, and it also helps rebuild trust and commitment in your relationship. No matter how small, each step is a step towards a stronger self and potentially a stronger bond.

Moving forward, we'll explore the impact of technology on relationships. In our next chapter, we will delve into how digital devices and social media can influence intimacy and connection, offering insights and strategies to ensure technology enhances, not hinders, your relationship. This following discussion promises to be an enlightening part of our ongoing conversation about navigating modern love with wisdom and wit.

FOUR

The Impact of Technology on Relationships

A h, technology! It's like that friend who always brings the coolest gadgets to the party but sometimes monopolizes all your time. In relationships, technology can be a fantastic bridge or a subtle barrier, depending on how we use it. Navigating our love lives in the digital age can be tricky and needs continued maintenance. So, how do we ensure our tech-savvy lifestyles enhance our relationships rather than hinder them? Let's dive into the complex world of social media and its impact on modern love.

Social Media: Connection or Disconnection?

Social media's role in relationships is a bit like a double-edged sword. On one hand, it can keep us connected with our partners through cute emojis sent during a hectic day or a funny meme shared to make each other laugh. It's like having a little digital bridge that keeps you connected even when you are miles apart. But beware, this digital bridge can sometimes become a battleground where jealousy and disconnection creep in, often without warning.

Think about the last time you scrolled through a social media feed and saw a post from your partner having a blast at a party you knew nothing about. It stings a little, doesn't it? Suddenly, questions appear like unwanted ads: Why wasn't I there? Who are those people with them? With its glossy showcases of perfect moments, social media can sometimes leave us feeling less than, doubtful, or even paranoid. This is where setting healthy boundaries comes into play. It's crucial to agree on what's cool to share online and what stays between you. Maybe it's deciding not to post certain pictures that have ex-partners in them or agreeing not to follow certain accounts that might trigger insecurity. Think of these boundaries like personal settings in your favorite app— they're there to make sure the system runs smoothly without any crashes.

Let's talk about transparency, the WiFi signal of trust in your relationship. Just as a weak signal can lead to a frustrating FaceTime call, a lack of transparency can lead to misunderstandings. Being open about who you connect with online and what you share helps maintain trust. It's like having an open browser history—nothing to hide or worry about. But remember, transparency works both ways; it requires both partners to be open, not just one.

And then there's the dreaded online conflict—when disagreements get typed out in a chat window, often blowing things out of proportion. Have you ever had a text argument escalate because you read their message in the wrong tone? Yep, we've all been there. Navigating these conflicts often requires stepping back and asking for a time-out—an in-person chat where you can read real faces, not just emojis. This approach can help clarify misunderstandings that are too common in the land of likes and shares.

Interactive Element: Social Media Agreement Template

Why not draft a Social Media Agreement to help you and your partner navigate the complex currents of online interactions? Sit together and discuss what makes you feel comfortable and respected online. Decide on privacy settings, sharing boundaries, and handling conflicts when they arise. Think of it as creating a user manual for your relationship in the digital world. This proactive step can prevent misunderstandings and ensure that social media remains a tool for connection, not a source of tension.

As we continue to explore the role of technology in our relationships, remember that, like any tool, its impact is all about how we use it. Stay tuned as we explore the digital dimensions of love, and find ways to navigate, enhance, and sometimes even limit our tech use to strengthen our connections, not strain them.

Digital Boundaries: Protecting Your Relationship Online

Digital boundaries serve as essential lines that help safeguard intimacy and privacy in relationships. Like in the physical world, where you wouldn't appreciate someone barging into your private moments without knocking, the digital world requires similar respect and boundaries.

Establishing these digital boundaries isn't about creating a fortress around your relationship but protecting it from unnecessary strain or drama that can seep in from unchecked online activities. When you set boundaries about who can see your posts or whose posts you engage with, you decide who gets a pass to your front row. This becomes crucial because social media and other digital platforms are rife with potential misunderstandings. For instance, an innocent like of an ex's photo, might seem benign to you but could create discomfort or misgivings in your partner. Here, it's not just about trust but respect and consideration for each other's feelings.

Negotiating these boundaries should be a cozy chat, not a boardroom negotiation. It's about finding a comfy spot, maybe over a cup of hot chocolate, and discussing what each of you considers private versus shareable. Maybe you're cool with your partner posting that goofy picture of you in a dinosaur onesie, but you might want to draw the line at sharing screenshots of your sweet nothing texts or sharing that photo of you dancing on a table like Coyote Ugly. It's all about giving each other a say in what feels right and what doesn't. It's not just about imposing rules but understanding and agreeing on them together, ensuring they fit snugly into your relationship dynamics without leaving anyone feeling policed or restricted.

Now, onto the digital intrusions—those little pings and notifications that can chip away at your couple time, turning what could be a moment of connection into a parade of pixelated distractions. Unchecked, these intrusions can create a feeling that you're just not present enough, engendering a sense of neglect. They subtly eat away at the quality of your interactions, making your partner feel less seen and heard. It's like trying to have a heartfelt conversation but with the TV blaring in the background—you're there, but not quite there. Setting specific times when you're both unplugged can create a sanctuary from these intrusions, helping foster deeper connections and making your together-time truly about each other.

Enforcing these boundaries with the outer circle—friends, family, colleagues—is equally vital. It's about gently but firmly setting expectations about your availability and engagement levels online with them. For instance, you might decide not to respond to work emails after dinner or to mute specific group chats that tend to blow up during your quiet time. It's about politely but assertively safeguarding your private time, ensuring that your digital life doesn't over-shadow your real-life moments together.

Navigating the digital landscape as a couple can sometimes feel like you're both learning to dance to a brand new tune—where every step and turn is a little unfamiliar. But with some thoughtful choreography in the form of digital boundaries, you can turn it into a dance that feels secure, respectful, and in sync with your relationship's rhythm. So, take the time to sketch out those lines in the sand and watch how they help keep your relationship's foundation solid, even in the ever-shifting sands of the digital age.

Using Technology to Enhance Your Relationship

Have you ever thought of technology as your relationship's assistant? Yeah, it's like having a super-efficient helper who keeps things running smoothly, ensuring you and your partner stay connected, no matter the distance or busy sched-ules. In a world where our phones often feel like an extension of our hands, exploring how these digital tools can bring us closer to the ones we love rather than just being a distraction is worth exploring.

Let's start with the basics—shared calendars and video calls. These aren't just for business meetings or keeping track of your dentist appointments. Imagine this: you and your partner have a shared digital calendar where you both pop in date nights, reminders for anniversaries (so no one forgets!), and even carve out times for heart-to-heart talks. This way, no matter how chaotic life gets, you have a clear view of the times you've dedicated to each other. It's like booking tickets to your private gig, where the main act is quality time with your favorite person. And video calls? They're a game-changer for long-distance relationships. They allow you to share moments in real time, showing off that new haircut or introducing them to your new adopted puppy. It's about sharing those everyday moments that text messages can't capture.

Let's dial up the fun with digital date nights and shared experiences. Think back to the last time you tried something new with your partner. Now, imagine doing that digitally. You could be on opposite sides of the globe and still watch the same movie simultaneously, pausing to debate over who's the best character or play an online game where you team up to take on virtual challenges together. It's about creating memories, even if you're not in the same physical space. You could even go on virtual tours of museums or exotic locations, exploring new cultures and learning new things, all while sharing screens. It's like an adventure in your pocket, waiting to be had.

Apps and platforms that promote a couple's growth are like the unsung heroes of relationship maintenance. These digital tools are designed to help you strengthen your bond through fun activities, challenges, and daily prompts that encourage communication. For instance, some apps send you daily questions to ask each other, which can range from silly to deep, helping you discover new things about each other or see different perspectives. Others might challenge you to complete little relationship-building tasks, like writing why you're grateful for your partner or sending them a photo of something that reminded you of them. These small gestures, facilitated by tech, can keep the spark alive and kicking.

In my guidebook, I mentioned 5 Categories of Self Care, which incorporate gratitude journaling. This is often an assignment I give to patients in various relationships. Whether for romantic relationships, friendships, or family relationships, this exercise helps with that deeper connection. I ask patients to print two copies of the following prompts and, in a journal, write answers to them and then exchange what they wrote with their significant other at the end of a week. So many times, patients report back to me saying, "I had no idea that this was so meaningful" or "I didn't realize that he/she had so much admiration for me or was proud of me." These positive words of affirmation go a long way. They build confidence in the other person, knowing that you love what they are doing, and want to repeat doing what they know you love. Individuals can sometimes be insecure about what makes them happy, and if you are often critical and give them no words of affirmation, they will start giving up and say, "I guess I don't do anything right!"

Gratitude Journal Prompts

- I was happy when my (significant other) did......
- The best part of time we spent together was....
- Something good my (significant other) did was.....
- My (significant other) made me laugh when......

- I was grateful for my (significant other) when.....
- Something my (significant other) accomplished was....
- My (significant other) helped me when....
- A challenge my (significant other) overcame was....
- I noticed one of my (significant other's) strengths when....
- I was impressed when my (significant other) did....
- Something memorable my (significant other) and I did was....
- Something fun my (significant other) and I did together was....
- I felt admiration toward my (significant other) when....

While plugging into technology has its perks, unplugging has its own set of benefits, too. Have you ever noticed how refreshing it feels to disconnect from all screens and be present with your partner? Maybe it's a lazy Sunday morning spent making pancakes and catching up or a quiet walk without the constant ping of notifications. These technology-free zones can help deepen your connection, making you feel more grounded and attuned to each other's presence. It's about finding that sweet spot where technology helps rather than hinders, enhancing your relationship while knowing when to turn it off and tune into each other.

So, as you navigate this digital age together, remember that technology is there to serve your relationship, not dictate it. Use it to enhance your connection, create new experiences, and make your relationship management smoother. But also cherish the moments of digital silence, where the only updates you're focused on are the ones in each other's eyes.

FIVE

Virtual Therapy: A New Frontier in Couples Counseling

W ho would have thought that one day, sitting in your pajamas with a cup of coffee in hand could be the new way to attend therapy? Welcome to virtual therapy, a game-changer for couples looking to enhance their relationship without stepping out the front door. The leap from traditional face-to-face sessions to digital screens might seem daunting, but it's like having a therapist in your pocket—ready when and wherever you are. This accessibility is significant, especially for those juggling hectic schedules or living in remote areas where a qualified therapist is about as familiar as a unicorn. Accessibility to virtual therapists can sometimes be limited because a therapist may only be licensed in specific States. A therapist who is only licensed in the State of New York for example cannot meet with you virtually and your partner if you traveled outside of New York to a different State or County for the day of the session. Both parties need to be in the same State. Inquire if your couples therapist can have flexible sessions and where both of you are located. Some companies cover therapists to virtually meet with you across the nation and around the world.

Now, let's stack it up against in-person therapy. Face-to-face sessions have charm and benefits, such as being in the same room can help foster a greater sense of connection and immediacy. However, virtual therapy brings its own set of advantages, especially in terms of privacy and comfort. Being in your own space can make opening up about deeply personal issues less intimidating. For some, the physical office of a therapist can be a barrier. Here, it is a reminder of the problems at hand. These defensive walls often lower naturally in your living space, leading to more open, honest dialogues. Yet, it's not all roses; virtual therapy can sometimes feel impersonal, and technical issues like a poor internet connection can disrupt the flow of a session, which can be frustrating.

Setting up a private, comfortable space is crucial to get the most out of virtual therapy sessions. This isn't just about physical comfort but creating a psychological safety zone. Choose a quiet corner of your home where you're unlikely to be interrupted. Consider using headphones for better audio privacy and to keep the conversation intimate. Good lighting and a stable internet connection also go a long way in enhancing the quality of the session. Think of this space as your sanctuary for healing and growth—a place where you can be open without fear of judgment or external interruptions.

Integrating the insights and exercises from virtual therapy into your daily relationship practices is where the magic happens. It's not just about those session hours; it's about taking what you learn and applying it to everyday interactions. Perhaps your therapist suggests a nightly gratitude exchange or a weekly check-in chat. These exercises can become rituals, strengthening your bond incrementally. Over time, this ongoing practice can transform your relationship, helping you to communicate more effectively, understand each other deeply, and navigate challenges with greater empathy and teamwork.

Virtual therapy is like having a guide on your relationship journey, accessible with the click of a button. It offers new possibilities for connection and growth, providing tools and insights that can be woven into the fabric of your daily life together. As you continue to explore and adapt to this digital method of strengthening your partnership, it offers just the right mix of convenience, privacy, and depth, tailored to fit the unique rhythm of your relationship.

Apps and Online Resources for Relationship Enrichment

Apps and online resources for relationship enrichment can be useful tools for cultivating a healthier, more connected relationship. Whether they enhance communication, add a pinch of fun, or provide deep insights into partnership dynamics, these tools are here to give your relationship care a modern upgrade.

Let's talk about the buffet of options available. Some apps turn relationship nurturing into a fun game where you earn points for sweet gestures or completing understanding exercises together. Think of it like those reward systems in video games, except the rewards here are real-life perks like a happier, healthier relationship. Then, there are communication tools that help you articulate your feelings more clearly, especially for those moments when the right words feel just out of reach. These apps often include prompts that guide you through expressing thoughts and feelings that might be tough to navigate.

Customizing these digital tools to suit your relationship's unique flavor is critical. Not every app or resource out there will fit your needs, and that's okay. It's about finding the ones that resonate with you and your partner. Maybe you're the couple who thrives on daily challenges and gamified apps, or perhaps you're more into deep conversations sparked by thought-provoking questions provided by a different app.

Balancing the use of these digital tools with in-person interactions is crucial. It's easy to get caught up in the convenience of technology, but remember, no amount of digital interaction can fully replicate the warmth of a handheld or shared hug. Use these tools to enhance your connection, not replace it. Schedule time for digital activities, but make time for unplugged moments together. Maybe decide that dinner time is a phone-free zone, or designate a tech-free day on weekends. It's about creating a balance that keeps the technology as a helpful assistant rather than the boss of your relationship.

Now, amidst all these digital opportunities, it's crucial to contemplate privacy and security. Just as you wouldn't leave your garden gate wide open, don't overlook the security settings on the apps and platforms you use. Ensure that your personal and relationship data are protected. This includes using strong, unique passwords for your apps, checking the privacy settings on each platform, and being mindful of what information you're sharing and who might have access to it. It's about protecting your digital relationship space with the same vigilance you'd protect your home.

Navigating the landscape of digital relationship tools can be an adventure. It's about exploring and experimenting with different apps and platforms to discover what works for your relationship. Like any good adventure, it comes with challenges and tremendous rewards. So, why not start exploring?

SIX

Basic Rules of Engagement

Disagreements can mean the difference between a healthy debate and a full-blown drama series in our living room. Establishing rules for respectful disagreement is like setting up the rules for a friendly board game; it ensures everyone knows what's fair play and what's out of bounds. One golden rule is avoiding absolutes. You know, those sweeping statements that start with "You always" or "You never." They're like throwing a match into a pile of dry leaves —likely to ignite a more significant fire. Instead, focus on the specific issue at hand. It's not about the person; it's about the problem. For instance, instead of accusing, "You never help around the house," try pointing out, "I feel overwhelmed when the kitchen isn't cleaned after dinner. Can we find a way to share this task more evenly?"

Basic Rules to Consider

1. Do some self-reflection before reacting: Are you really that upset that your partner forgot to get toilet paper, or are you upset because your partner should take better inventory and repeatedly puts you and your family at risk of needing to use leaves from outside as TP? Recall the reference to **Four Horsemen and Antidotes**.

Example of how Not to frame your interaction: "You always forget to get toilet paper! Why are you so incompetent?" This is an example of using horsemen of criticism and contempt, and your partner will most likely mirror your Horsemen with Defensiveness or stonewalling. How is this productive? Nothing gets resolved; you're more angry with each other and still out of TP!

Example suggestion of what to say: "I am noticing that we are dangerously low on the TP, and I am wondering if there could be a better way for us to do inventory before getting to this point? Maybe we could make a list of items that usually need to be replenished every month, and have a reminder set on our phones to add those items to grocery list each month?"

2. Please address just one topic at a time: Apply assertive communication, clearly state how you feel about something, and discuss ways to help the situation moving forward. You don't want to bring up something that annoys you and then proceed to bring up multiple other annoyances that happened months ago or even years ago. Your original point gets lost in the sauce, and absolutely nothing gets resolved because both of you are frustrated.

3. Don't be hurtful, condescending, call each other names: Remember that these behaviors are Horsemen, and if this continues to be a standard way of communicating with each other, your relationship will be irreparably damaged over time. Remember antidotes. How can we show respect and love while discussing ways to improve and grow? We stay calm, don't raise our voices, call each other names, but listen to each other reflectively and talk solution-focused ideas.

4. Effective communication with words: Expressing your needs assertively can make a world of difference. Keep it on the "I." **The assertive communication formula to remember is to respect** yourself and the other person, state clearly your needs and wants, and provide solution-focused ideas or compromises.

Example of what not to do: "You never kiss me goodbye. You must not care about me!"

Example of more effective communication: "I feel sad when you don't kiss me goodbye in the mornings before going to work. That's a tradition I grew up with to show love and care. Could we make it a habit to kiss each other goodbye in the mornings?" "

5. Do reflective listening and take turns speaking:

This may seem awkward initially, but put a timer on and give each other 2 minutes to say your peace. During these two minutes, you should not think of comebacks or reasons you are upset. During these two minutes, you actively listen to the other person and attempt to gain perspective. With reflective listening, you need to summarize what you think you heard the other person say as best you can.

Reflective listener summary example: "It sounds like you were frustrated and just wanted to vent and didn't want my feedback or for me to fix anything. Is that right?"

By summarizing what you think you heard, you show that you are trying to listen and be as empathetic as possible. The other party, instead of being on the defensive, is on the offensive and thinks, "Wow, he/she is trying to understand me. I appreciate that. Let me further clarify."

6. If you are too upset, don't just walk away!

Be mindful of personal indicators that you are getting upset. Are your hands shaking, your voice quivering? Is your heart beating fast? Are these signs that you are overwhelmed and may say something you will later regret? As you notice signs, verbalize this as calmly as possible, and state that you want to resume the conversation later.

Example of how Not to frame your interaction: Say something you regret or just shut down and walk away. Either option will lead to further divide and escalation in the situation.

Example suggestion of what to say: "I am feeling a little overwhelmed and upset right now. Let me take a breather and a long walk. I know it is important that we talk through this, so let's plan to meet in an hour, come back calmer, and have some solution-focused ideas to improve this situation. "

Finding compromise and common ground might sound like a political negotiation strategy, but it's just as applicable in love as in politics. It starts with both partners acknowledging that a relationship is a partnership, not a battleground. Each conflict presents an opportunity to forge stronger bonds by finding solutions considering both sides. This doesn't mean you split every difference down the middle—compromise can also look like taking turns in concessions or even coming up with a third, entirely new path forward. It's about understanding and respecting each other's needs and finding ways to meet in the middle that feel fair to both of you. So next time you disagree, try to step into your partner's shoes and look for that win-win. It might not always be easy, but the strength of your relationship will grow with every compromise you make together.

Navigating conflicts with fairness and respect isn't just about maintaining peace; it's about enriching your relationship and making it more resilient and understanding. By setting clear rules, taking breaks when needed, communicating openly and effectively, and seeking compromise, you and your partner can turn every disagreement into an opportunity to learn more about each other and deepen your connection. Remember, the goal isn't to avoid conflict but to manage it in a way that strengthens your bond, proving that sometimes, it's not the disagreements that define us but how we handle them.

Identifying Underlying Issues in Conflicts

It's like seeing just the tip of an iceberg when conflicts arise. What you're arguing about might be visible, but there's usually a more significant, deeper issue lurking underneath the cold water. For instance, a fight about unwashed dishes could be about someone feeling undervalued or overburdened. Understanding this can change the entire dynamic of how you and your partner approach resolutions.

Digging into these underlying issues requires some detective work and lots of honest communication. Start by asking yourselves what bothers you about the situation.

Now, let's talk about using conflicts as mirrors—reflective tools that help us see not only our partners but also ourselves more clearly. When a conflict arises, try to see it as an opportunity for self-reflection instead of gearing up for battle. Ask yourself, "What is this disagreement teaching me?" It could be patience, understanding, or needing to be more upfront about your feelings. Transforming conflicts into opportunities for personal growth can turn them from relationship roadblocks into stepping stones.

A tool I often share with patients is the Anger Iceberg diagram. Imagine an image of an iceberg, and the tip of the iceberg is anger, but just underneath the surface are so many very different emotions. I ask patients if any of the following emotions resonate with them.

- Scared
- Annoyed
- Sad
- Overwhelmed
- Embarrassed
- Hurt
- Attacked
- Pain
- Frustrated
- Disrespected
- Worried
- Grief
- Anxiety
- Stress

- Threatened
- Tired
- Guilt
- Jealous
- Nervous
- Shame

I had a patient that held so much contempt for her husband and was so frustrated with how he would get angry with any purchase she made, big or small. After reviewing the other emotions, the patient was able to acknowledge that he could be experiencing anxiety and stress due to significant debt and is scared of not being able to provide for his family and not being able to protect his family from bankruptcy. I encouraged pt to suspend judgment and apply empathy when interacting.

Example dialogue: "Hey, I know that you are stressed about our debt, and the input of funds is not as much as the output. How can we cut some costs and have certain caps for certain spending each month?"

I go into further detail about financial stress in Chapter 10; however, a suggested tool I often recommend to patients is YNAB.com. It is both a website and an App, which has been clutch for many patients. It is user-friendly and makes the old Excel sheet method much more relaxed and less scary. Couples can jointly use it and see visually how they are doing month to month financially. They can see areas where they can cut costs areas where they are saving, and get a better picture of timelines for financial goals.

Past experiences and personal baggage can heavily influence how we perceive and react to situations in our relationships. Maybe leaving dishes undone in your family was a sign of disrespect, or perhaps your partner grew up in a home where chores were distributed unevenly, or they needed to be the sole provider and be entirely in charge of all finances. Recognizing these influences can open up new pathways for understanding each other's reactions that aren't just about the moment but are rooted in a lifetime of experiences. These behaviors can also be learned to create more harmonious relationships. It's about being open to finding the right balance for your unique relationship to reinforce that greater emotional and physical connection.

Conflict De-Escalation Exercise

Here's a simple yet effective exercise to help uncover underlying issues in conflicts: next time a dispute arises, take a moment to write down what you think the fight is about. Then dig deeper—ask yourself what emotions you're feeling and why. Share these insights with your partner and ask them to do the same. This can lead to surprising revelations about what's at the heart of your disagreements and guide you toward more constructive, empathetic conversations.

By shifting focus from the immediate triggers of conflicts to their deeper roots, you and your partner can address the real issues at hand, making your conflict resolution sessions not just about finding peace momentarily but building a deeper understanding and intimacy in the long run. Remember, the goal isn't to eliminate conflicts—because, let's face it, that's about as likely as finding a phone charger that lasts a lifetime—but to transform how you deal with them, turning each disagreement into a bridge rather than a barrier.

After the Storm: Reconnecting After a Fight

After the dust settles and the echoes of a heated argument fade, there's often a palpable tension that can feel as thick as pea soup. What you do in these moments can either set the stage for a sequel nobody wants to star in or become a healing balm that strengthens your bond. One of the first steps towards reconciliation is making repair attempts. Think of these as little bridges you build to reconnect with your partner. These could be as simple as a gentle touch on the arm, a small joke to lighten the mood, or a heartfelt "I'm sorry" that shows you care more about your relationship than winning an argument. The magic of repair attempts lies in their ability to deflate tension and show openness to resolution. They signal clearly: "I want to fix this, not because I have to, but because I want to." This proactive approach can prevent resentment from festering and turning your home into a silent battleground.

Acknowledging each other's perspective is another cornerstone of post-conflict connection. It's about stepping into your partner's shoes. Validating doesn't mean agreeing—recognizing that their feelings are valid and understandable, given their viewpoint. For instance, saying, "I can see why you felt ignored when I didn't answer your texts during the meeting," acknowledges their feelings without conceding your stance. This validation can be incredibly soothing and is often all needed to begin mending fences. It's about affirming that you respect and value their experiences and emotions regardless of the disagreement.

Let's talk about rebuilding intimacy because conflicts can leave our emotional closeness feeling a bit threadbare. Small gestures and activities can be wonderfully effective in restoring this connection. Something as simple as making your partner a cup of coffee in the morning or leaving a sweet note on the fridge can speak volumes. These actions, small as they may be, are like stitches mending a tear, subtly reinforcing the fabric of your relationship. You might also consider setting aside some time for an activity you both enjoy: a walk in the park or a bowling night. It's not just about the activity itself but the message it sends—I'm here, with you, and committed to us.

Reflecting on disagreements as growth opportunities can transform the way you view conflicts. Instead of seeing them as roadblocks, view them as stepping stones to deeper understanding and more robust connection. After a disagreement, take a moment to reflect together on what triggered the conflict, how it escalated, and how you both responded. This isn't about assigning blame but learning and growing together. What did you discover about each other's triggers or sensitivities? How can you both adjust your behaviors to support each other better? This kind of reflection not only helps prevent similar conflicts in the future but also deepens your mutual understanding and appreciation.

Reflective Pause

To foster this learning, try setting aside time after you've both calmed down from a fight to discuss what happened. Approach this conversation with curiosity rather than criticism, aiming to understand rather than to judge. This can help turn even the most painful arguments into valuable lessons that strengthen your bond.

As we wrap up this exploration of reconnecting after conflicts, remember that every couple has disagreements. What sets strong relationships apart is not the absence of conflict but the ability to navigate these rough patches and come out stronger on the other side. By making timely repair attempts, validating each other's feelings, investing in small reconnecting gestures, and learning from each experience, you and your partner can restore your connection and enhance it, making your relationship more resilient and understanding.

Our next chapter will focus on deepening emotional intimacy, a fundamental aspect of any strong relationship. We'll explore how nurturing this dimension of your partnership reinforces that connectedness and overall happiness together.

SEVEN

Emotional Intimacy: The Heart of the Matter

E motional intimacy requires ongoing nurturing to flourish. It's not just about big romantic gestures or deep heart-to-heart talks under the stars. The real magic happens in the everyday moments, the little routines that might seem mundane but are the glue holding your relationship's mosaic together.

Daily Rituals to Strengthen Emotional Bonds and Understand Each Other's Love Languages

Now, let's talk about the power of daily rituals. These are your morning coffees, "how was your day" debriefs, or those evening walks after dinner. Think of them as mini-dates; they don't require much time but need your presence (so maybe don't scroll through your phone the whole time). Remember that is also the Love Language of **Quality Time.** Establishing these rituals creates a rhythm of togetherness, ensuring that, despite the chaos of daily life, you have these touchpoints that bring you back to each other.

Consider the simple act of having coffee together every morning. It's not just about the caffeine fix; it's about starting your day connected. You share the first thoughts of the day, maybe plan, or just enjoy the silence together. It sets a tone of partnership and priority: before the world rushes in with its demands, you choose to pause and connect. Over time, this small ritual becomes a cornerstone of your relationship, a daily reaffirmation of your commitment to each other. My now-husband understood this concept early on in our relationship, and even though he despised the Cafe Bustelo coffee that I made, he drank it with me for months until he finally came clean after feeling confident that I wasn't going anywhere. We compromised on the coffee but not the morning rituals, and it definitely is a staple of our relationship.

Now, let's sprinkle in some small gestures. These tiny acts of kindness and love often go unnoticed but are incredibly potent. A love note tucked into a laptop bag, leaving fresh cut flowers on the dining room table, a supportive text before a big meeting, or even taking over a chore your partner dislikes when they're having a tough day. Coming home early from work and instead of plopping on couch, playing soccer with the kids or prepping for dinner. These acts might seem small, but they're mighty. They communicate, "I see you, I appreciate you, and I'm here for you," without needing to shout it from the rooftops (though feel free to do that too, if you're so inclined). These gestures show the love languages of **Acts of Service and Gift Giving**. When the other partner notices these gestures and shows appreciation, it reinforces positive feelings towards each other that you want to continue replicating.

Cultivating a Culture of Appreciation

Creating a culture of appreciation in your relationship can transform the mundane into something profound. Regularly expressing gratitude and appreciation isn't just about good manners; it's about reinforcing the value you see in each other. It's easy to overlook each partner's everyday contributions, especially when life gets busy. By saying "thank you" for the small things—whether it's for making coffee, running errands, or being a great listener—you acknowledge the effort your partner puts into the relationship. This recognition builds a foundation of respect and appreciation that can elevate your connection, and it also reinforces the love language of **Words of Affirmation.**

Finally, the role of traditions cannot be overstressed. These aren't just the extensive holiday rituals or anniversary celebrations and the tiny, personal traditions you create for the two of you. Maybe it's a quirky game night every Friday or an annual day where you both ditch work and go golfing. These traditions become the unique fingerprints of your relationship, creating a shared history that only you two fully understand. They reinforce a sense of 'us' against the world, deepening your bond and giving you something special to look forward to. In a way, traditions are the stories you write together, each one strengthening the narrative of your life together.

Reflective Journaling Exercise

Take a moment to think about the daily rituals, small gestures, expressions of gratitude, and traditions in your relationship. Write them down, and reflect on how they might impact your emotional connection. Are there new rituals you'd like to introduce? Are there gestures or words of appreciation you wish to express more frequently? This exercise isn't just about awareness; it's about improving your relationship.

In weaving these daily practices into the fabric of your life, you're not just passing the time together; you're actively building and reinforcing the emotional intimacy that can sustain your relationship through the ups and downs of life. It's about finding the extraordinary in the ordinary, the magical in the mundane, and, in doing so, creating a relationship that is as rich in intimacy as it is in love.

Sharing Your Inner World: Dreams, Fears, and Hopes

Opening up to someone about your deepest fears, wildest dreams, and sincerest hopes can feel scary. It's vulnerable, yes, but so important to share. Think of it this way: sharing these personal insights is like handing over the roadmap to your inner world. It invites your partner to understand you on a deeper level and nurtures a closeness that superficial conversations can't touch. This depth of sharing can transform your relationship, turning casual companionship into a profound connection that withstands the tests of time.

But how do you create a space where it feels safe to open up about things often kept under lock and key? It starts with the environment you cultivate with your partner. Imagine setting a stage where both of you can speak your truths without fear of judgment or dismissal. This means actively practicing empathy and patience, ensuring that when your partner says, their words aren't met with criticism or contempt but with understanding and openness. It's about confirming their hopes and fears are as valid and vital as yours. Creating this type of environment requires consistent effort. It involves actively listening, not just hearing. When your partner reveals something personal, focus on their words entirely. Put away distractions, maintain eye contact, and ensure your body language conveys your interest and care. This non-verbal cue can sometimes speak louder than any words of reassurance.

Now, let's talk about the magic of sharing goals and dreams. Working towards something together, be it as monumental as buying a house or as simple as planning a weekend getaway, creates a shared sense of purpose. These shared goals act like glue, bonding you together in unique ways. When you cheer each other on towards individual aspirations or buckle down together to achieve a common goal, you're doing more than just sharing tasks. You're reinforcing your partnership, celebrating each other's strengths, and compensating for each other's weaknesses. This incredible thing happens when you realize you're each other's cheerleader; it deepens your bond in palpable and subtle ways.

Navigating fears and uncertainties together is equally crucial. Life throws curveballs, and sometimes those curveballs can be scary. Whether it's concerns about job security, health, or family issues, facing these fears with your partner can make them seem less daunting. The key here is not only to see fears but also to sand other through them actively. This support might look like discussing contingency plans, offering reassurance through difficult times, or simply being there as a sounding board. It's important to remember that this support should be reciprocal. A give and take happens; sometimes, you're the one offering the shoulder to lean on, and at other times, you're the one leaning. This dynamic balance is what keeps the relationship grounded and strong.

As you and your partner share more of your inner worlds, you'll likely find that your relationship deepens unexpectedly and beautifully. This isn't just about being open but about being open-hearted. It's about allowing your partner to see all parts of you, the good and the not-so-good, and loving each other all the more for it. It's about building a bond that isn't just about weathering storms together but celebrating sunshine and chasing rainbows together. So, take the leap, open up, share more, and watch your relationship blossom into something truly magnificent. Our next chapter will delve into the Love Language of **Physical Touch**.

EIGHT

Reigniting Physical Intimacy

Physical intimacy—just the phrase can send shivers down your spine or, sometimes, a wave of anxiety. Whether you're in the honeymoon phase or have been partners in crime for decades, maintaining that spark can feel like trying to keep a campfire going in the rain. It's not just about stoking the fire; it's about understanding why sometimes it feels like you're using wet logs. Here, we dive into the cozy, sometimes blush-inducing world of physical intimacy, not just to rekindle that fire but to turn it into a lasting blaze that lights up your entire relationship.

Communicating Desires: A Guide to Vulnerable Conversations

"Let's talk about sex, baby!". Yes, communicating about your physical desires is probably up there with singing karaoke in terms of vulnerability. You're on stage, the mic is hot, and your heart's beating out of your chest. But here's the thing: opening up about what you want, need, or dream about in your physical relationship can be the key to maintaining intimacy and deepening it.

Initiating these conversations requires courage and a good dose of honesty. Begin by creating a safe space where you and your partner feel comfortable expressing your desires without judgment. This could be a relaxed date night at home, a quiet moment after dinner, or any time you feel connected and undistracted. Approach the conversation with an open heart and a curious mind. Instead of launching into a monologue about your needs, start the dialogue with an invitation for mutual sharing. Try kicking things off with something like, "I've been thinking about how we can make our time together even more amazing, and I'd love to know what you think, too."

Navigating feelings of embarrassment or shame that might bubble up during these chats is crucial. Remember, these emotions are entirely normal. Everyone has them, and they don't have to be conversation stoppers. Acknowledge them with humor and compassion—maybe say, "I'm feeling a bit like a teenager talking about this, but.......!" This can lighten the mood and show your partner that expressing themselves freely is okay. The goal here isn't just to share but to share openly and without self-judgment. Another suggestion is maybe gifting a sexy outfit, and see if that stirs up conversation. "So, you want me to wear only a Firefighter bib and hat?"

The Role of Non-Verbal Cues in Expressing Desires

While words are powerful, let's not forget the silent language of love—our non-verbal cues. These can be just as eloquent in conveying desires. A gentle touch, a lingering look, or even the way you move can communicate volumes about your feelings and desires. Be mindful of your body language during these conversations. Are your arms crossed, or are you physically turned toward your partner, making eye contact? These signals can either invite closeness or build walls. Try mirroring your partner's posture or leaning in slightly to show your engagement and interest in the conversation. These subtle cues can turn a good talk into a great one, where both of you feel seen and understood.

Creating a feedback-friendly environment is the final piece of the puzzle. This is about making it clear that feedback is accepted and appreciated. Encourage your partner to share their thoughts and feelings about the conversation, and be open to adjusting your approach based on their feedback. You might say, "I want to ensure this is comfortable and enjoyable for both of us. What are your thoughts? How was that for you, were you completely happy and comfortable?" This kind of open dialogue can help refine your communication over time, making each conversation more accessible and more fulfilling than the last.

Opening up about your physical desires isn't just about improving your sex life; it's about deepening your connection to each other in one of the most intimate aspects of your relationship. By approaching these discussions with honesty, openness, and a readiness to listen, you can transform them from potentially awkward moments into opportunities for growth and connection. Remember, the goal is to understand better and fulfill each other's needs, enhancing your physical intimacy and overall relationship. So take a deep breath, grab that metaphorical karaoke mic, and let your heart sing. Your relationship will be all the richer for it.

Overcoming Barriers to Physical Intimacy

Imagine this: you're all set for a romantic evening. The mood is right; the lights are dimmed, but then, out of nowhere, it feels like an invisible wall between you and your partner. It's not made of bricks or stone but is just as accurate. This wall could be built from stress, health issues, or maybe an emotional disconnect that's crept in so quietly you hardly noticed. Recognizing these barriers and addressing them is imperative.

First up, let's talk about stress. It's like the junk mail of life; it just keeps coming no matter how often you toss it in the recycle bin. When stress from work, family, or daily hassles piles up, it can dampen your desire and make physical intimacy feel like a chore rather than a pleasure. Identifying stress as a barrier is the first step. Once you see it, you can start managing it, maybe with some meditation or just ensuring you both carve out time to unwind together. It's about turning those individual stressors into a collective de-stressing session, transforming tension into relaxation.

Health issues, too, can play a significant role. Whether it's a chronic condition, fatigue, or even side effects from medication, these physical challenges can stealthily steal away your intimacy. Facing these together, rather than as isolated battles, can help. Sometimes, it's about adjusting expectations or finding new ways to connect physically to accommodate challenges. This could mean more cuddling, massages, or simply holding hands more often. Remember, intimacy is not just about the grand gestures; it's also found in the small, quiet moments.

Reconnecting emotionally is essential for breaking down the disconnect. This might involve more heart-to-heart conversations, spending quality time together, or engaging in activities that both of you love. It's about rediscovering each other and reminding yourselves why you fell in love in the first place. Emotional intimacy fuels physical intimacy; it's the heart that pumps life into the physical aspect of your relationship.

Working Together to Overcome Intimacy Challenges

Tackling these barriers as a team can turn challenges into bonding opportunities. It's about pulling together, not pulling away, when things get tough. Start by setting a regular 'us' time, where you can talk about what's working and what's not without distractions. Use this time to brainstorm solutions or plan to address any issues head-on. Maybe it's scheduling regular date nights, planning a weekend getaway, or simply having a quiet evening at home. The goal is to ensure both partners feel involved and invested in overcoming the barriers together.

Even when you're doing your best, it's okay if the path forward isn't clear. In such cases, seeking professional help can be beneficial. A therapist or counselor can provide new perspectives and strategies that you might not have considered. They can assist with navigating complex issues such as deep-seated emotional disconnects or communication breakdowns that could impact your physical intimacy. Seeking help is not a sign of defeat; it's an act of strength and commitment to each other and the relationship.

Addressing these barriers to physical intimacy openly and together helps reinforce that your partnership is strong, resilient, and adaptable. It's about acknowledging that while the physical aspect of your relationship is essential, it's deeply intertwined with emotional and mental well-being. By supporting each other through these challenges, you strengthen your bond, making your relationship more fulfilling both in and out of the bedroom.

Innovative Exercises to Rekindle Passion

It's all about stepping out of the routine and trying something new together. So, let's roll up our sleeves and dive into some innovative exercises that can sprinkle a little extra spice into your love life.

First up, why not try a sensual massage? It's not just about kneading away those knots—it's a chance to connect on a sensory level. Set the scene with dim lighting, soft music, and maybe a hint of your favorite essential oils wafting through the air. As you explore the contours of your partner's body, let your hands communicate care and affection. This touch can speak volumes, conveying love and desire without a word. It's a relaxing way to reconnect physically and can be a profound act of intimacy that recharges your body and your emotional bond.

Or how about shaking things up with a dance class? Whether it's salsa, tango, or hip-hop, dancing together can be an exhilarating way to reignite that physical spark. It's all about moving in sync, anticipating each other's steps, and maybe even laughing through missteps. Each dance, each step, and turn brings you closer—literally and figuratively. Dancing boosts your physical connection and rekindles the joy and playfulness in your relationship, reminding you both of the early days when everything was exciting and new.

I may be biased towards dance as I grew up in the dance world. My godmother was the late Katherine Dunham, a world-renowned dancer, anthropologist, author, and humanitarian. Dance was integrated into all areas of my life, especially the spiritual and emotional sense. So when my husband, on one of our earlier dates at a dance club, without hesitation, took my hand and gracefully led me to dance to some Latin music, that emotional connection locked in step with that physical connection.

Exploring New Dimensions of Intimacy

Now, let's talk about exploring new dimensions of intimacy. This could be anything from experimenting with new romantic ideas to embracing aspects of fantasy and play. The key here is mutual consent and comfort. Start with an open conversation about fantasies or new things you both might be interested in trying. It could be role-playing, new settings, or perhaps a little adventurous scenario you both feel safe exploring. This openness can significantly deepen trust and enhance your intimate connection, bringing a fresh layer of excitement and closeness to your relationship.

Building anticipation is another thrilling way to enhance intimacy. Surprise your partner with a mystery date where only you know the details, or send them on a scavenger hunt that ends in a romantic picnic. The anticipation of something exciting can be incredibly alluring. It's like the build-up to a beautiful surprise, where the excitement bubbles up with each passing moment. These surprises don't have to be grand; sometimes, surprising your partner with a planned date night can rekindle feelings of romance and appreciation, filling every moment leading up to it with delightful suspense.

By incorporating these innovative exercises into your relationship, you're not just maintaining the spark; you're feeding it, letting it grow and evolve. Whether through the intimate touch of a massage, the synchronized rhythm of dance, the thrilling venture into new romantic territories, or the playful suspense of anticipation, each activity offers a unique pathway to rekindle and enrich your physical connection. So, why not leap?

As we wrap up this chapter on reigniting physical intimacy, remember that keeping your relationship's romantic and passionate aspect vibrant requires creativity, openness, and a willingness to explore new ideas together. These exercises are just the beginning—invitations to continually rediscover and reinvent your intimate connection, ensuring it remains as exhilarating and profound as ever.

The next chapter will focus on maintaining autonomy within your relationship. We'll explore how fostering individual growth and respecting personal space can paradoxically bring you closer, enriching your relationship with trust and independence.

NINE

Personal Growth Within the Relationship

What secret ingredient keeps relationships vibrant and growing, even after decades? Spoiler alert: it's not just endless love or grand romantic gestures—it's also about each partner's personal growth. Let's dive into how growing individually fulfills you and brings fresh energy and a richer perspective to your shared life.

The Journey of Self-Discovery Together

I strongly encourage you to review my first guidebook, "5 Categories of Self Care: The Ultimate Guide to Finding Self Love and Happiness." I help guide the reader in assessing how much they care for themselves physically, emotionally, socially, spiritually, and professionally. I always tell my patients that if they are independently happy and love themselves and their partner is also independently happy, then they can elevate each other's happiness and not become co-dependent. You can complement each other's strengths and reinforce your love and admiration for one another. Engaging in this journey with your partner can transform your relationship into an exciting adventure. Imagine both of you bringing back treasures from your quests of self-discovery—new interests, skills, or insights—and sharing these to enrich your collective life. This exchange keeps the relationship dynamic and exhilarating, preventing that dreaded feeling of staleness that can creep into long-term relationships.

Supporting each other's self-discovery is akin to being the best cheerleaders for each other. It's about celebrating when your partner wants to take up a new hobby, pursue a new career path, or even revisit an old dream that was shelved. Partners genuinely supporting each other's journeys creates a deep trust and appreciation. For instance, if your partner decides to take up writing and is excited about publishing their first book, showing genuine interest and appreciation for their effort encourages them to continue exploring their new passion. It's these moments of support that deepen your bond significantly.

Shared Growth Experiences

Now, how about syncing your growth journeys? Engaging in activities or challenges together can be a fantastic way to grow individually and as a couple. This could be anything from taking a cooking class to joining a dance studio or even challenging each other to read several books each month. These shared experiences not only bring fun and laughter into your relationship but also true joy.

Finding the right balance between individuality and togetherness can be challenging. It's essential to cherish and support each other's interests while ensuring you spend quality time together. This balance is crucial; too much focus on particular activities can create distance, while too little can stifle personal growth. Striking this balance ensures that both partners feel fulfilled individually and as a couple. It's not about sacrificing your growth for the relationship or vice versa; it's about harmonizing the two in a beautiful, ever-evolving dance.

Reflective Journaling Exercise

Grab your journal and reflect on these questions: What new interest or passion would I like to explore? How can I support my partner in their growth journey? What activity can we start together that will help us both grow? Writing down these answers can clarify your thoughts and spark meaningful conversations with your partner about your individual and collective growth paths.

Embracing personal growth within your relationship is about giving each other the space to grow, supporting each other's journeys, and finding joy in learning and experiencing new things together.

Encouraging Each Other's Goals and Dreams

Imagine your relationship as a team sport. You're not just spectators cheering from the sidelines; you're both in the game, passing the ball, making plays, and scoring goals together. In the game of life, these goals often translate into personal ambitions and dreams. When you actively support each other's aspirations, you're not just boosting each other's chances of success but reinforcing the foundation of your partnership. Think of it this way: every cheer, every bit of encouragement, and every strategy discussion not only pushes the individual forward but strengthens the bonds that keep you connected as a couple.

Now, let's chat about the magic that happens when you align your individual goals with your relationship goals. It's like syncing your playlists so that both of your favorite tunes harmonize into a perfect road trip soundtrack. When your personal aspirations and relationship directions complement each other, it creates a sense of unity and shared purpose. This alignment doesn't mean you have to give up your dreams for the sake of the relationship; instead, it's about finding ways your dreams can coexist and support each other. For instance, if one of you dreams of returning to school to change careers, how does that fit with your shared goals of financial stability or starting a family? Finding common ground might involve planning out timelines that accommodate both your education and your family planning, or it might mean temporary sacrifices that benefit the long-term health of your relationship. It's about weaving your dreams together so that neither feels sidelined, but instead, both feel propelled forward.

Celebrating each other's successes is crucial. It's easy to cheer when the times are good, and the achievements are rolling in. However, the real test is maintaining enthusiasm for small victories that might not seem monumental but are steps toward a bigger goal. Did your partner finally sign the papers to officially become a Partner of his/her firm? Throw a mini-celebration. Did they get up half an hour earlier all week to fit in a workout? Make a big deal out of it with breakfast in bed on the weekend. These celebrations don't just make your partner feel loved and appreciated; they reinforce the idea that you are in each other's corner, no matter how big or small the victories. Each celebration reminds you why you fell in love and what you admire about each other, reinforcing the emotional support under_ying your physical and romantic connection.

Navigating differences in ambitions can seem daunting, but the goal is to respect each other's dreams by finding creative ways to support them, even if they don't perfectly align with your own. It's about crafting a relationship environment where both partners feel they can pursue their passions without fear of losing support from the other. This balance of giving and taking, understanding and adjusting, can turn differing ambitions from potential relationship hurdles into opportunities for growth and mutual support.

Fostering a relationship where both partners feel empowered to chase their dreams creates a dynamic, supportive, and deeply fulfilling partnership. It's about more than just staying in love; it's about growing in love, side by side and step by step, as you each reach for your dreams and celebrate the journey together. So, keep those cheers loud, the support firm, and the compromises creative, and watch as your paths weave a more robust, more vibrant tapestry of shared life.

Balancing Autonomy with Intimacy

Sometimes, the fear of losing oneself in a relationship is genuine. It's like slowly fading the volume of your favorite song until it's just background noise. Many of us worry about this. We fear that in loving another, we might forget to love ourselves or lose those quirks that make us. Addressing these fears starts with open communication—clearly expressing your needs and boundaries. It's about saying, "I love us, and I love me, and I need a little space to nurture that love." It's not selfish to seek personal space; it's necessary. A little solitude, a hobby that's just yours, or even moments of reflection are like breaths of fresh air that rejuvenate your spirit and enhance your ability to engage and connect with your partner.

Practical strategies for maintaining autonomy while fostering intimacy might sound like a tightrope walk, but it's pretty achievable with some mindfulness. Start by establishing and respecting personal boundaries. Discuss with your partner what alone time looks like for each of you. Is it an hour with a book, going to the gym, a solo walk, trivia night, karaoke with the girls, or a local winery with friends? Respect these needs in each other without guilt or resentment. Encourage and celebrate the pursuit of individual passions and hobbies. Seeing your partner lit up about their interests is attractive and adds intriguing layers to your conversations and shared life.

The dynamic interplay between autonomy and intimacy is fascinating. Balancing well fosters a relationship where both partners feel secure yet free, connected yet independent. Regular check-ins help maintain this equilibrium, ensuring both partners feel fulfilled individually and together.

In embracing autonomy and intimacy, you're not setting up divisions but strengthening the bonds that hold you together. By supporting each other's independence, you build a deeper trust and appreciation that enriches your shared life. This approach enhances personal fulfillment and injects a healthy vitality into the relationship, keeping the romance and connection alive and thriving.

In the next chapter, we will discuss managing external stressors. We'll explore how financial stress in your relationship can impact your romantic life and discuss strategies to shield and strengthen both of you in the face of life's inevitable challenges.

TEN

Financial Stress: Navigating Together

L et's talk money—I can almost hear the collective groan! Money issues are like that one guest who overstays their welcome at parties, lingering awkwardly long after the music has stopped. It's no secret that financial stress can crank up relationship tension. The key to handling this uninvited guest? Open and honest conversations about finances.

Start by setting a "money date"—a relaxed, scheduled chat where you can discuss your finances openly without judgment. This isn't about pointing fingers or assigning blame for that extra splurge on a fancy rocking lounge chair with an umbrella with cup holders. Instead, it's about understanding each other's financial perspectives, goals, and worries. It's about finding common ground in a territory that often feels like a minefield. Transparency is your best friend here; it builds trust and prevents those minor misunderstandings from becoming Mount Everest-sized obstacles.

Creating a Joint Financial Plan

Now, let's go on to crafting your financial battle plan! Think of it as drawing a treasure map where X marks the spot of your shared financial goals. Whether saving up for a dream vacation, buying a home, or just ensuring you don't end up eating instant noodles at month's end, having a plan can make all the difference. Start by outlining your major expenses, then look at where you can realistically save. Maybe it's cutting back on certain subscriptions or opting for cooking in versus ordering Uber eats regularly. A tool I often share with many of my patients is an App/website called YNAB.com, which stands for You Need a Budget. (Full disclosure: I am not being paid to discuss this company.) So many patients come back to me excitedly and often say, "Ynab app has been a Game-Changer for us!" The app/tool makes financial planning fun and brings your regular Excel spreadsheet to life. You visually see timelines for meeting specific financial goals. You set the financial allocations as paychecks come in, and you see it immediately allocated to particular objectives: saving for a trip, saving for school expenses, saving monthly costs for utilities, rent/mortgage, groceries, subscriptions, etc. You can also see where you can cut costs or where you are in the red. But it is gratifying to see that money is not just going into the abyss but is working towards your financial goals. This automatically decreases stress and decreases financial tension within couples.

The Role of Financial Counseling

If the numbers start to look more like ancient hieroglyphics, it might be time to call the cavalry—financial advisors. These wizards of wealth aren't just for the ultra-rich; they're for anyone who wants to manage their money smarter. Think of a financial advisor as a guide who helps you navigate the murky waters of finances, providing clarity and peace of mind. They can offer personalized advice tailored to your financial situation and help you both understand complex financial jargon. Investing in professional guidance can pay off massively by setting you on a path to financial security, making it a worthy consideration for any couple feeling overwhelmed by monetary matters. If you're looking for a referral, I recommend looking into MGE Legacy Wealth Advisors. MGE Legacy Wealth Advisors | Financial Advisor | Williamsville, NY (MGElegacywealth.lpl.com) MGE Legacy Wealth Advisors takes a holistic approach by creating a personalized strategy to help manage your current and future financial needs. Whether in your life's later stage(preservation and income) or the beginning stage(wealth building), MGE will help create a tailored plan to help reach your personal financial goals.

Balancing Financial Goals and Relationship Health

Remember, while money is necessary, it's not the glue that holds your relationship together. Don't let your financial goals overshadow the love, respect, and joy you share. It's easy to get caught up in the numbers game, but at the end of the day, the moments of laughter, the quiet evenings together, and the mutual support through life's ups and downs truly enrich your relationship. Keep the lines of communication open, support each other's financial aspirations, and ensure that your emotional connection remains the richest asset in the ledger of life.

I remember watching a stand-up routine by Nate Bargatze and him mentioning something so accurate. He said that you will have a dreamer and a realist in relationships. If you have two dreamers in the relationship, you will be broke. My husband endearingly calls me the dreamer, and he is both the realist and financial advisor in the family. I have huge dreams, and costs are more of an afterthought. My husband helps ground me by saying, "Though I love the idea, I am not sure it is practical and within our budget. We must prioritize school tuition over a three-week vacation to Greece." We have had different opinions when it comes to finances, however, we have navigated stress through reflective listening and finding compromises.

Navigating financial stress together requires teamwork, transparency, and creativity. Treating your finances as a joint venture, where both partners have equal say and respect, you turn potential conflicts into opportunities for growth and deeper understanding. So, grab those financial bullhorns by the horns, set your sights on your goals, and dance through the money rain with confidence and a shared vision. Together, you can survive the financial storms and thrive, crafting a future that's as prosperous as it is happy.

If you love this book so far, please consider making a difference with your review!

I want to make "The Evolution of Single Life to Life Partnership" accessible to everyone, and I need your help spreading the word.

Most people judge a book by its cover (and its reviews).

Your generous gift of leaving a positive review could help single individuals and couples worldwide and change their lives forever.

Thank you in advance for your consideration!

Katherine Ibarra

ELEVEN

Dealing with Extended Family Dynamics

Navigating extended family can be challenging—the cast members of our life's sitcom can either bring comic relief or a bit of drama. Whether it's the slow in welcoming sister or brother-in-law, soon-to-be in-laws, the interrogating aunt, or the cousin who is adamant that you are not good enough, navigating these relationships can be as tricky as juggling flaming torches. Family dynamics can inject unnecessary stress into your relationship, turning your duo into a crowded dance floor where everyone's steps seem out of joint. Recognizing the potential for these pressures and facing them head-on with grace and strategy is essential for maintaining harmony at the family table and in your relationship.

So, how do we best navigate these relationships? First and foremost, setting healthy boundaries is critical. Consider boundaries not as barriers but as guidelines that help your family understand how to love and support you without overstepping. It's about respectfully communicating what is and isn't acceptable. For instance, you might decide that Sunday dinners are a delightful tradition, but unexpected weekly drop-ins are a no-go. Or perhaps you're okay with discussing your career aspirations but draw the line at invasive questions about when you'll have kids. It's all about clarity—making sure that everyone knows where the lines are drawn, which helps prevent misunderstandings and conflicts.

I also emphasize the importance of understanding cultural backgrounds and customs when first meeting a family and extended family. Doing preemptive research could significantly save you from making that first impression a nightmare.

For example, I grew up in two very different backgrounds. I lived in the United States for the school years, and Summers and Christmases, I lived in Port Au Prince, Haiti. For me, one custom in the US was to say "good morning" and ask how the other person slept. In Haiti, the customs are very similar to those in France in that you greet everyone with a kiss on both cheeks and say, "Bonjour! Comment as-tu dormi?." One morning in Haiti, I did not greet one of my aunts with two kisses and say "bonjour." Boy, was I in trouble. This was a great insult and a big no-no. So, I share this story to tell you that if you meet the family on a weekend camping trip or have dinner at their home, or go to a very fancy gathering; make sure that you ask your partner everything there is to know about their family's cultural boundaries, customs. How do they greet each other? If it is a fancy restaurant do you know all of the silverware placement and when to use them? Does the family do a prayer before eating? Does everyone wait for everyone to have food on their plate and seated before eating? Or is it very casual, buffet style where people get their plates and sit wherever? They may have very different cultures/customs than yours, but at least showing respect and attempting to engage with those customs will help you be accepted into the new family much more smoothly. Some basic etiquette suggestions though that will be appreciated across all cultures. When meeting family at their home: Bring a gift—flowers. wine, or a box of pastries. Thank the family for inviting you, and what a pleasure it is to finally meet them in person. Ask if you can help at all in preparing for the meal. Always offer to help clean up. Whether they accept or decline the offer, they will be impressed that you offered.

Establishing a United Front with Family

Presenting a united front with your partner when dealing with family is like showing up to a potluck dinner with a well-prepared dish—you both need to agree on what you're bringing to the table. This unity shows your family that you support each other's decisions and boundaries. which can discourage any attempts to create divisions between you. For example, if a family member criticizes your partner, standing together in defense reinforces your solidarity with each other and your family. It's not about creating conflict; it's about showing that you're both singing from the same song sheet when it comes to your partnership. Consistency in this united front is crucial; it sends a clear message of mutual respect and support, strengthening your relationship's resilience against external pressures.

Navigating holidays and other family gatherings can often feel like planning a military operation—strategic and sometimes a tad stressful. The key to managing these events lies in setting clear expectations beforehand. Discuss with your partner what you anticipate and dread about upcoming gatherings. Maybe you decide together that you'll only stay for three hours at the family BBQ or skip the stress of the midnight countdown at New Year's in favor of a quiet evening at home. Whatever your strategies, the goal is to make these decisions as a team. This ensures that you're both on the same page and helps mitigate the stress of assumptions or last-minute choices.

Communication and Compromise with Family

Effective communication and the willingness to compromise are your best tools when dealing with different family dynamics. It's about navigating those moments when your uncle starts a heated political debate, or your sister begins to pry into your financial status. Here is a gentle but firm redirection that can work wonders. A simple "Let's talk about something a bit lighter" or "We're focusing on the positive tonight" can steer conversations away from potential landmines. On the compromise front, sometimes agreeing to disagree can preserve peace without anyone feeling like they've compromised their values or beliefs. It's about finding the middle ground where respect is maintained, and everyone feels heard—even if not everyone agrees.

Handling extended family dynamics with finesse involves setting boundaries, presenting a united front, managing expectations, and mastering the art of diplomatic communication. By tackling these challenges head-on, you and your partner can prevent external pressures from casting shadows over your relationship, ensuring that your bond remains strong and your gatherings stay cheerful. So, next time you find yourself at a family event, remember these strategies. With a bit of patience and understanding, you can navigate the intricate dance of family dynamics with grace, keeping your relationship's melody sweet and harmonious.

TWELVE

Work-Life Balance: Setting Boundaries

Navigating work-life balance in the modern age. It's no newsflash that the stress from our jobs can sneak into our homes like uninvited guests. and they're not the best party companions. Establishing clear boundaries between your professional and personal lives is like setting up a good, sturdy fence—it helps keep the peace. It ensures that work stress doesn't trample over your relationship's beautiful, well-maintained garden.

Think about the last time your workday seeped into family time. You may check emails at dinner or mentally rehearse a presentation while your partner shares something meaningful. It's easy to let these moments slide, but they can accumulate like unwashed dishes, and we all know how that story ends. Setting boundaries might mean turning off your work phone after a particular hour or dedicating a 'no work talk' zone during meals. It's about creating physical and mental spaces where work is not allowed to intrude, ensuring that when you're home, you're fully present. This isn't just beneficial for your relationship; it's also a massive part of professional self-care and mental health.

Now, onto the sweet stuff—prioritizing quality time together. In the relentless hustle of our routines, it's crucial to carve out oases of 'us time.' This means consciously planning regular date nights, weekend getaways, or even quiet evenings with a board game or a puzzle. These moments are the anchors that keep your relationship steady in turbulent waters. Think of this dedicated time not as a luxury but as essential maintenance for your relationship.

Communicating About Work Stress

Keeping stress bottled up is like shaking a soda can—it will burst at some point. Open dialogue about work-related stress can be incredibly freeing. It's not about offloading your problems onto your partner but sharing your burdens. Sometimes, simply verbalizing what's on your mind can lighten your load and help your partner understand what you're going through. They might not have solutions, and that's okay. Often, just being heard is enough. Encourage this dialogue by asking each other, "How was your day?" and listening to the answer. This habit can turn what's often a conversational autopilot mode into a genuine, supportive exchange.

Strategies for Achieving Balance

Achieving work-life balance doesn't come with a one-size-fits-all solution, but a few strategies can universally help. Time management is critical. This might mean organizing your day so that high-priority work tasks are tackled when you're most productive, leaving your evenings free of the most demanding work. Also, consider delegating responsibilities at home. Splitting chores, planning meals, and scheduling downtime can prevent one partner from feeling overwhelmed. Remember, your home life should be a collaboration, not a solo project.

By setting boundaries, prioritizing quality time, openly communicating about work stress, and employing practical strategies to manage daily life, you create a healthier balance that benefits your relationship and overall well-being. It's about making sure that at the end of the day, you can leave work at the door and step into a home that feels like a sanctuary, not just a sleep station.

THIRTEEN

Navigating Life Changes

L ife changes are expected and unexpected at times, sometimes thrilling, and often a test of character. And when it comes to relationships, these twists can be the ultimate test. Common life changes can be becoming new parents, health issues, or moving to an entirely new location. First, we will discuss the joys, adjustments, stressors, and challenges of becoming new parents.

The Transition to Parenthood

Parenthood is not just about adding a member to your family; it's a profound shift that can shake the very foundations of your relationship if you're not ready to jiggle and wiggle together through the seismic shifts. It's about learning to dance to a new rhythm that includes diaper changes at 3 AM and finding ways to keep the spark alive even when you're both running on fumes.

Maintaining intimacy and partnership in the whirlwind of new parenthood is crucial. It's easy to get so wrapped up in your roles as new parents that you forget about being the partners who started this adventure. One key strategy is to carve out time for just the two of you. It might sound like a luxury when you're knee-deep in baby gear, but it's essential. This could be as simple as enjoying coffee together in the morning while the baby naps or watching a movie after bedtime. It's not about grand gestures but finding moments to reconnect as partners, not just as parents.

Keeping the lines of communication open is another vital part of maintaining your connection. Parenthood can feel like you're building a plane while flying it, and it's easy to feel overwhelmed. Regular check-ins where you can talk about more than just baby-related topics can help. Use this time to express concerns, share feelings, and reassure each other. Remember, it's okay to admit that you're finding things tough. These honest conversations can help prevent resentment and ensure you feel supported and understood.

Sharing parenting responsibilities is not just about fairness; it's about teamwork. It's easy for one partner to do more child-rearing than the other, leading to burnout and bitterness. Tackling this head-on involves clear conversations about dividing responsibilities in a way that feels fair to both of you. Maybe you take turns doing the night feeds, or one handles mornings while the other covers evenings. The key is flexibility and openness to adjusting the plan as you go along because what works one month might be a disaster the next. Treat it like a dance where sometimes you lead, and sometimes you follow, but you're constantly dancing together.

Navigating changes in identity can be one of the subtler yet profound challenges of becoming parents. You're not just you anymore; you're also someone's mom or dad, and that shift can stir up feelings about who you are and who you want to be. It's essential to give each other space to explore these new identities. Support each other's interests and passions, both old and new. Encourage your partner if they want to take up a new hobby or go back to an old one. Remember, growing as an individual allows you to bring more to your relationship, enriching it with new energies and inspirations.

Embracing parenthood is about more than just adjusting to a new family member; it's about adapting to a new way of being together. It's about finding joy in the chaos, leaning on each other, finding humor, and continuing to nurture your relationship amidst the sea of diapers and sleepless nights. By supporting each other's growth, sharing the load, and carving out time for your partnership, you can make this transition a chapter of deepening love and commitment. So, grab your partner's hand, look into each other's sleep-deprived eyes, and step into this new adventure with hearts wide open and a spirit of teamwork ready to take on the world—one baby step at a time.

Self-disclosure: My husband and I started having children two years after marriage. We had time to be a married couple, get more situated in our careers, be foodies, go out with friends, and travel. We wanted kids but weren't fully prepared and financially ready. I remember my husband one day telling me after an Uber ride that the driver gave him some solid life advice. He said the driver, who had five children, told him that having children if you can have children, is one of the greatest joys in life. My husband told him, "I am not sure we're ready financially," the driver told him it will never be the perfect time; you just have to trust that it will work itself out. That driver said precisely what my husband needed to hear to take that leap of faith. Having children was one of the best decisions of our lives. We knew that life would change. However, we fully embraced it.

After having my first child in 2016, I was determined to still go to restaurants and travel, and I would find creative ways to bring the baby. Our firstborn was low maintenance, and we took her everywhere in her little Doona. We even took her to France when she was a little over a year old, and she was able to meet some of my family members as well as an old classmate of mine from Germany who came to visit us in Paris.

I share this to say that it is important not to view life with the fear of uncertainty and anxiety of specific barriers after having children, but a beautiful change in life that you adapt to and apply your strength of creativity in navigating these new and exhilarating adventures.

Now, we will talk about the life change of moving to cities or even to different countries. Whether for a job, family, or just a change of scenery, relocating is like doing a trust fall with your life; it requires more leaps of faith, a lot of teamwork, and, yes, a great sense of humor. So, let's unpack this suitcase of challenges and opportunities and help you navigate your move without turning your love story into a stress saga.

Moving: A Test of Unity and Adaptability

Moving is like starting a new season in your relationship docuseries—new characters, new settings, and new plots await. This can be both a stressor and an opportunity. On one hand, you're leaving behind the familiar—friends, family, your favorite coffee shop. On the other, you're embarking on a fresh adventure together, which can dial up your relationship's unity and adaptability levels.

Strategies for a Smooth Transition

First thing first: communication is your best packing tool. Start by sitting down with your partner to map out the move. This isn't just about deciding which furniture to cut; it's about discussing your hopes, worries, and expectations. Who will handle the utilities switch? When should we send our resignation letters in for work? Who's in charge of the farewell party? Splitting tasks not only lighten the load but also prevents resentment from one partner taking on too much. Remember, it's about moving together, both physically and emotionally.

As a young couple pre-kids, we were able to survive and love almost everything NYC had to offer, but after having two kids, the reality was we were bursting at the seams in our one-bedroom apartment in Harlem. The thought of navigating strollers up and down subway stairs and or paying astronomical amounts towards daycare was not appealing. I started looking at 2-bedroom apartments in the area, and prices on the low end were $800,000. I asked my husband, "How in the world will we ever be able to save after shelling out just basic expenses for groceries, rent, utilities, and daycare?"

My brilliant and loving mom sadly died many years before I even got married and had kids, and we did not have family locally to help us. My incredible mother-in-law and father-in-law kept reminding us, "If you move to Buffalo, John and I can help with the kids." My husband is originally from

Orchard Park, NY, and early on in our dating years would bring me to Buffalo to visit for various events or the holidays. I fell in love with Buffalo and everything it offers. Whether it is reasonable cost of living, wholesome place to raise a family, outstanding public and private schools, great food with their wings and beef on weck, a fantastic passion and spirit for the Buffalo Bills, and being 30 minutes away from crossing the border into Canada, it finally dawned on me, "Why not move to Buffalo?" My husband's initial response was, "Really?! You want to move to Buffalo?" Then we started talking about why it made so much sense, and we became super excited about the idea. We knew there would be many challenges in navigating out of NYC with careers and roots we established over the years, but we were up for the challenge and had our eyes set on a better life in Buffalo.

It is crucial for couples to keep the connection lines open during a big move. It's easy to get caught up in packing boxes and managing movers, but remember to check in with each other. A simple "How are you holding up?" or "Need a break?" can go a long way. It's like keeping your phone charged—ensuring you don't run out of juice when needed.

Building a New Support Network

Once you've landed in your new residence space, it feels like being the new kid in school all over again. Building a new support network is crucial. Start exploring together—join local clubs, take classes, invite neighbors over for BBQ, or spend time in community spaces like parks or coffee shops. For parents, a great way of meeting new people is through their children's schools, daycare and attending meet and greet or child activity functions. Each new friend or acquaintance is a potential new adventure. And remember, it's okay to lean on your partner more than usual during this time. Think of your relationship as a portable charging station—you can offer each other energy and support no matter where you are.

Maintaining Connection During the Move

Constantly remind each other of the reasons behind the move. Whether it's a better job, a more pleasant climate, or the lure of adventure, revisiting these motives can help keep spirits high.

Keep the spark alive by turning this shared challenge into fun. Why not turn unpacking sessions into dance parties or explore your new neighborhood with photo challenges? Documenting these moments can turn a stressful move into a memorable chapter in your relationship story. For those of you who move from a city to a much slower-paced suburb, it is the little things really that excite us. For one, just being able to park your car at the grocery store and then drive your groceries to the front door of your home is such a novelty for city dwellers. In the city, we had to use a stroller to lug groceries or hold very heavy groceries for multiple blocks to our apartment, and then enter the apartment complex and walk up the steps to our apartment. Thankfully, we lived on the first floor but just think of those without elevators who live in walk-ups. Yes, it is a good workout, but with a small family, having a little convenience is everything. I remember my husband and I on a daily would laugh as we reflected on how much easier life was in the suburbs, and say "Why did we torture ourselves for so long in the city?"

Interactive Element: Relocation Reflection Exercise

Before you get lost in the sea of cardboard boxes, take a moment for this quick reflection exercise. Grab a piece of paper and jot down answers to these questions:

1. **What are three things I'm most excited about in our new city?**
2. **What are three challenges I anticipate, and how can we tackle them together?**
3. **How can we make our new place feel like 'home' together?**

This exercise can help clarify your thoughts and ensure you're both on the same page. Plus, it's a great way to keep the excitement alive amidst the stress of moving.

Navigating the move to a new city is a test of unity and adaptability for any couple. But with the right strategies, a focus on maintaining your connection, and a willingness to dive into building a new community, you can turn this life change into an enriching adventure. Keep your sense of humor handy, hold onto each other, and get ready to set up a home in a new location and a new chapter of your lives together. So, pack up your bags (and your patience), and let's make this move another reason to celebrate your partnership.

Career Changes and Relationship Dynamics

Let's talk about a roller coaster that doesn't involve an amusement park but can be just as thrilling and stomach-churning as career changes. Whether landing a dream job, facing a layoff, or diving into a completely new field, shifts in our professional lives can ripple through our relationships unexpectedly. Suddenly, your daily routines, financial stability, or even your roles at home might need a serious reshuffle.

First, let's tackle the emotional whirlwind that can come with these changes. If your partner is stepping up the career ladder or jumping into a new industry, it's a mix of excitement and anxiety. Here's where your cheerleading skills come in handy. Offer affirmations that are specific to their situation. For instance, if your partner is nervous about managing a larger team, remind them of when they organized that big family reunion, and everyone raved about how well it was handled. It's about spotting those transferable skills and boosting their confidence. On the flip side, if they're dealing with job loss, help them see it as a setback and a potential slingshot into new opportunities. Encourage them to explore passions or interests that might open up new career avenues. Your role? Be the sounding board, the brainstorming buddy, and sometimes, the chief motivational speaker.

Beyond the pep talks, practical support is crucial. This might mean taking on a bit more around the house if your partner burns the midnight oil at a new job or temporarily adjusting the budget to accommodate a dip in income. It's like you're both crew members on a ship; when one needs to man the helm, the other might need to hoist the sails. The smoother you can make these transitions for each other, the less turbulence you'll feel in your relationship. Also, consider setting up a weekly check-in, not just to discuss how things are going but to connect emotionally. These moments can be your relationship's anchor, keeping you grounded and connected no matter how choppy the seas get.

Balancing career ambitions with relationship goals can sometimes feel like plotting two courses on a map. Here's where the art of compromise and alignment comes into play. Sit down and map out your career trajectories and how they intersect and influence your shared goals. Maybe one of you has a job that requires relocating every few years while the other is tethered to a specific location. Finding a middle ground might involve pursuing remote work opportunities or seeking jobs in a new city that offers potential for both careers. It's about weaving your dreams into a shared tapestry that neither stifles one's aspirations nor sidelines the other's.

Communication and Reassessment of Roles

As for household and relationship roles, these need a creative overhaul as careers shift. If one partner's new job means more travel, the other might need to take on more at home, or outsourcing some tasks is the way to go. This is where clear, honest communication plays a starring role. Discuss expectations, acknowledge frustrations, and be open to tweaking arrangements as needed. It's not about keeping score but finding a flow that works for both of you, ensuring that neither feels overwhelmed or underappreciated.

Navigating career changes together requires emotional support, practical adjustments, and continuous communication. It's about being each other's coach, teammate, and cheerleader all rolled into one. By actively supporting each other through these transitions, you manage to keep your relationship strong and build a deeper understanding and appreciation for each other's professional journeys.

As we wrap up this chapter on navigating significant life changes, remember that whether it's moving cities, becoming parents, or shifting careers, these transitions are not just challenges to be managed but opportunities to grow closer and strengthen your bond. Each change is a chance to turn towards each other, adapt, and build a more prosperous, more fulfilling life together. Up next, we'll explore unique relationship dynamics. From long-distance relationships to blending families, we'll dive into how couples can navigate these situations with love, patience, and creativity.

FOURTEEN

Unique Relationsh p Dynamics

P icture this: your relationship is a thrilling book series, each chapter filled with adventures, twists, and turns. Now, we're turning the page to a chapter many dread, yet others embrace long-distance relationships (LDRs) with hope and excitement. The notorious LDR is often viewed like the cliffhanger at the end of your favorite season—exciting yet nerve-wracking. But fear not! Whether you're oceans apart because of a new job, school, or just the cruel twist of fate, let's navigate these uncharted waters with humor, a dash of creativity, and heaps of understanding.

Long-Distance Relationships: Staying Connected

Physical Distance Presents Unique Challenges

So here you are; your love feels very much tested. The physical distance between you and your partner can feel like a vast ocean. Waves of loneliness might hit, or storms of doubt may brew, questioning if your ship will reach the shore. But let's anchor ourselves for a moment. The main squalls to weather here are communication and trust—without these, any relationship can drift off course.

Maintaining honest and open communication is your lifeline. It's not just about frequent talks but meaningful exchanges that bridge the distance. Share the mundane details and the significant moments. It's about creating a sense of shared daily experiences, like sending a photo of the quirky street performer you saw or a quick voice note saying you miss their terrible jokes. Though seemingly small, these moments are the building blocks of trust and intimacy in an LDR.

Trust that words of affirmation hold so much weight and become even more crucial when navigating different time zones instead of just zip codes. It's about being reliable, whether calling when you say you will or being transparent about your feelings. The trust you build can make the distance seem less daunting, and the relationship feel more secure.

Importance of Planning Regular Visits

Now, let's talk about the heart of long-distance relationships: the visits. Planning regular in-person meetups is imperative. These visits are the highlights, the moments you'll mark on your calendar in bold. But they're more than just countdowns; they're essential for maintaining a tangible connection, a reminder of why the miles are worth it. Each visit can reinforce your bond, reignite the spark, and give you both memories to hold on to during the lonelier days. Plus, anticipating seeing each other can add an exciting edge and leave you with utter excitement and anticipation.

Leveraging Technology to Stay Connected

For the old-school romantics, the ink-to-paper love letters are significant, but in the modern-day world, technology is a friend, too. Today, technology is the unsung hero of long-distance relationships. It bridges the gap, making the world feel smaller with every text, call, or video chat. Virtual dates can be a game-changer. You can watch the same movie simultaneously, take a virtual museum tour, or even cook the same meal together over a video call. These activities help maintain a sense of normalcy and shared experiences vital for feeling connected.

Use technology creatively. Apps that allow you to watch videos together or play games online can add an element of fun and make it feel like you're sharing the same space, even if it's just digital. And let's not forget good old-fashioned emails or letters; sometimes, pouring your heart out in writing can be incredibly romantic and a beautiful keepsake for the future.

Even those simple little text messages can be significant. Be mindful of the thoughtful messages between the funny memes and mundane conversations. When your partner says, "I miss you" or "I love you," be considerate when responding. Try not to just click on the "Thumbs up" emoji, but at least put in the energy to click on the "heart" Emoji. The added effort of responding with a similar sentiment with actual words would also be very much appreciated.

Another suggestion for individuals in their early stages of dating. Be consistent with correspondence. For example, you have been sending a morning text every morning for the past three weeks, and suddenly, you don't text at all one morning due to a busy morning work schedule. The other party may jump to wrong conclusions and create unnecessary anxious thoughts. Just give your partner a heads-up. For example, "Hey, tomorrow, I will be going to work super early and will have back-to-back meetings until late. Maybe we can touch base when I get home tomorrow night?"

This may seem like a small, insignificant gesture, but it is very significant as you are reinforcing a healthy and secure attachment style with each other.

What are attachment styles? Let's review.

Knowing your attachment styles within relationships is a good barometer of your type of thinking and behavior. An individual with a secure attachment style completely trusts a partner, can effectively communicate needs and wants, and is not dependent on the other individual. A person with insecure attachment tends to be easily jealous, anxious, and worried about their bond with their partner and fears being abandoned.

Secure Attachment: This person is already independently happy in life. Has self-confidence and trusts partner. The individual is fully engaged and present emotionally and physically.

Insecure Anxious Attachment: Needs to be around partner 24-7; if not, they will be worried that their partner will leave or is cheating on them. This individual is uncomfortable with emotions and conflicts and cannot express needs and wants clearly.

Insecure Avoidant Attachment: This individual is uncomfortable with emotions and conflicts and tends to be very distant and detached as a defense mechanism. They tend to avoid situations in which they feel vulnerable, intimate, and committed.

Anxious-avoidant attachment: This type of attachment may present with extreme opposite emotions. The person may want intimacy with their partner but distrust intimacy and have difficulty maintaining healthy boundaries. They also gravitate to regular high-conflict engagement.

These are learned behaviors from childhood and early adult experiences. Attachment styles can be influenced positively or negatively. Ideally, both of you come into the relationship with secure attachment styles, which makes for an almost seamless and in-sync relationship

If you have a secure attachment style and your partner has an insecure attachment, your actions and behaviors can encourage your partner to become more secure. It will take some time for both of you to be harmonious, and your partner will need to unlearn learned behaviors and adopt more secure traits.

Suppose both of you have insecure attachment styles due to previous traumatic past relationships or bad experiences in childhood. In that case, you both may find yourselves reinforcing insecure traits and developing a more toxic and codependent relationship.

I always tell my patients about relationships that you have to love yourself before you can love anyone else. You need to be independently happy in life.

When two independently happy individuals find each other, they complement each other's strengths and elevate each other's happiness. This makes for a very sustainable relationship. You continually support, love, respect, and appreciate each other always and forever.

Transitioning to or from Long-Distance Relationship

Transitioning into or out of a long-distance phase can be like moving from one climate to another; adjusting takes time. Whether starting a long-distance relationship or closing that distance, it's crucial to set expectations and discuss how this change might affect your dynamics. Talk about what communication will look like, how often you'll visit, and your end goals. This clarity can prevent misunderstandings and ensure that both partners are on the same page.

Remember, every long-distance relationship is a journey of its own. With the right navigation tools—trust, communication, and a bit of creativity—you can turn this challenge into a testament to the strength and depth of your bond. So, let's keep the lines open, the visits frequent, and the love flowing. Here's to making those miles insignificant compared to the feelings you share.

Blended Families: Building New Bonds

Imagine you're crafting a recipe from two different cookbooks; each has its unique flavors and traditions. Now, you're trying to blend them into one delicious meal everyone at the table will enjoy. That's a bit like blending families. You have a mix of personalities, histories, and expectations all coming under one roof. It's not just about hoping everyone gets along —it's about actively crafting new family dynamics that honor each person's uniqueness while forging a cohesive family unit.

Navigating the relationships with stepchildren and ex-partners often feels like being a diplomat in an intricate maze of diplomacy. Each step must be measured; each word must be weighed for its impact. The first thing here is to establish a foundation of respect and patience. Children may not understand why things are changing and might not be ready to give their approval just yet. They need time to adjust and see that you respect their feelings and existing relationships, especially with their other biological parent. It's crucial to affirm their feelings, validate their emotions, and let them know they're heard. For example, when introducing new family traditions, why not include them in the decision-making process? Ask what they'd love to add to the holiday celebrations or a family game night. This inclusion can make a world of difference in helping them feel valued and heard rather than feeling like they're being forced into a new family mold.

When it comes to ex-partners, keeping things civil is critical. This isn't just about making your life easier—it's about modeling maturity and respect for the children. They need to see that adults can manage differences and work together, even when they're no longer in a relationship. Clear, respectful communication with your partner's ex can set a powerful example for everyone involved. It shows that despite the changes, the focus remains on the well-being and happiness of the children. This might mean setting up boundaries around communication—deciding what's shared, when, and through what channels—to avoid misunderstandings and ensure that conversations remain productive and respectful.

Establishing New Family Dynamics

Creating a new family dynamic is less about enforcing new rules and more about building a new culture to which everyone contributes. It's about finding a balance where old traditions are honored, and new ones are embraced enthusiastically. Start with regular family meetings where everyone can voice their thoughts and feelings about how the family is blending. Maybe one child feels left out, or another is confused about the new living arrangements. These meetings can be a safe space to air grievances and collaboratively find solutions. They can also be a time to celebrate wins, no matter how small, like a week without arguments or a successful family outing.

In these dynamics, patience isn't just a virtue; it's a necessity. Blending families is a process filled with ups and downs. There will be days when it feels like two steps forward, three steps back. But with each challenge comes the opportunity to learn more about each other and grow closer as a family. It's about taking the long view and recognizing that while the blending might be tough now, you're laying the groundwork for a loving, supportive family environment that will stand the test of time.

Maintaining Couple Intimacy Amidst Family Blending

In the whirlwind of blending families, it's easy for your relationship with your partner to slide onto the back burner. But here's the thing: the strength of your couple's relationship is the cornerstone of your newly blended family. Prioritizing your partnership is crucial, not just for your happiness but for the stability it brings to the entire family. Make it a point to schedule regular date nights, even if it's just a coffee together before the day begins or a walk after dinner. Use this time to connect as partners, not just as co-parents. Discuss your feelings, dreams, and challenges. Keeping your bond strong provides a secure base for the entire family.

Communication and Boundary Setting

Clear communication and firm boundary-setting are the guardrails that keep the blended family on track. Discuss openly with your partner how you will handle discipline, what roles each of you will play, and how you will manage conflicts when they arise. You must be on the same page and present a united front to all the children. Consistency in these areas can help prevent a lot of confusion and conflict.

Setting boundaries also extends to managing time and space within your home. Each family member should feel they have personal space and time. This can be particularly important for children who may feel they've lost a sense of privacy or control over their environment. Encourage everyone to respect each other's personal belongings and spaces, and make sure there are clear rules about knocking on doors, sharing items, and respecting privacy.

Navigating the complexities of blending families is undeniably challenging, but it's also an opportunity to build something beautiful and enduring. With patience, understanding, and open communication, you can create a supportive and loving blended family that stands strong together.

FIFTEEN

Age-Gap Relationships: Bridging the Differences

Age-gap relationships—the romance that can raise eyebrows. But here's the thing: Age-gap relationships bring unique challenges and perks. Navigating these can be akin to mixing a vintage wine with a vibrant cocktail— delightful and offering an exquisite blend when paired thoughtfully.

Exploring Challenges and Celebrating Benefits

Let's crack open the book on age differences. Often, it's not just the years that separate you but the cultural references, the life experiences, and, sometimes, the life stages. Each of these elements can color your relationship with different shades. For instance, one of you might be in the throes of career-building while the other is pondering retirement. Such differences aren't just numbers; they're whole chapters of life that you might read at different paces. Finding common ground or creating new spaces where these different chapters can merge seamlessly is crucial. This might involve aligning your daily routines in ways that respect both of your current life focuses or finding shared hobbies that bridge the age divide, turning what might be a gap into a gateway for mutual growth and enrichment.

Now, onto the societal spotlight—yes, those not-so-subtle stares or the awkward questions at family gatherings. Facing societal judgments can feel like you're constantly defending your love story. The key is to weave a narrative of strength from your unique relationship dynamics rather than viewing it through a lens of defiance. When faced with external skepticism, anchor yourself in the reality of your relationship. Communicate openly about how these perceptions affect you and strategize on handling them with a united front. Whether deciding how to address intrusive questions or support each other through the discomfort, remember that you, not the world outside, define your bond's strength.

Aligning Life Goals and Values

Aligning life goals and values in the face of age differences requires honest conversations and sometimes creativity. It's about ensuring that both partners feel their aspirations and needs are valid and considered. Open communication is your best tool here. Discuss each other's vision for the next five, ten, or twenty years. Are there discrepancies in where you see yourselves? How can you bridge these differences? Perhaps it involves compromise or taking turns in supporting each other's goals. For instance, if one dreams of traveling extensively and the other is concerned about the timing due to career commitments, planning shorter, more manageable trips could be a way to honor both desires. It's about crafting a shared future that respects both of your dreams, creating a vibrant tapestry with the threads of your aspirations.

Let's not forget the perks! Age-gap relationships can be incredibly enriching. The blend of wisdom and fresh perspective can be a powerful catalyst for personal growth. Older partners often bring a wealth of experience and a calming presence, while younger partners can inject vitality and a new zest for life. This exchange can be invigorating, challenging each of you to see the world through a different perspectives. Celebrate these differences. Let them be reasons for admiration and appreciation. Share your worlds—introduce each other to your favorite music, books, or life philosophies. Each shared piece strengthens your connection and deepens your understanding of one another.

In age-gap relationships, like any good book, every chapter offers something valuable. Embracing the challenges and celebrating the unique benefits can transform your narrative from differences to profound unity. So, cherish the diversity of your experiences and let them enrich your journey together.

SIXTEEN

Communication Gamechangers

E ver felt like your daily chats with your partner are more like two ships passing in the night rather than a cozy coffee chat? You're not alone. It's so easy to fall into a routine where "How was your day?" gets a "Fine, and yours?" response, and that's the end. But let's spice things up and turn this routine on its head. Consider the "How Was Your Day?" game—your new go-to method to exchange words and truly connect and add an extra layer of intimacy to your everyday interactions.

The "How Was Your Day?" Game

Imagine transforming your usual, perhaps mechanical, daily exchange into a meaningful ritual that builds the foundation of your communication castle. Here's where deep listening and sharing come into play, turning mundane moments into gems of emotional connection. In this game, you and your partner take turns diving into the highs and lows of your day without interruptions. I will say that uninterrupted time with small children is virtually impossible, but let's say you find some time somehow. Try to show you are fully engaged and listening; do not chime in with your stories; check your phone. It's about creating a space where you feel heard and valued, knowing your partner genuinely is listening to whatever you say.

This simple yet profound act of sharing and listening does wonders. It pulls you out of autopilot mode, which many of us switch on during daily conversations. By focusing on the details—the small win at work, the frustrating phone call, the micromanaging boss, the toxic co-worker, or even the weird lunch you had—you open up new avenues to understand each other better. This isn't just about updating each other about your day and showing empathy and support. It's like saying, "I see you, I hear you, and what you experience matters to me." This enhances your emotional connection and strengthens your bond over shared experiences and mutual understanding.

But wait, there's more! Integrating this game into your daily routine does wonders for your overall communication. It sets a tone of openness and attentiveness that can make tackling more complex, perhaps even thorny, conversations much smoother. Think about it—if you're used to listening and empathizing with the small stuff, you're better equipped to handle more significant issues with patience and understanding. It's like training for a marathon; you start small, build your stamina, and before you know it, you're tackling the big miles together with less huffing and puffing.

Interactive Element: Daily Debrief Exercise

To get you started, here's a little exercise. Set a timer for just 5 minutes each evening, sit down with your partner, and ask each other, "How was your day?" Take turns sharing while the other listens without distractions and body language also show engagement. After sharing, spend a couple of minutes summarizing what you've heard. Try your best not to try to solve or "fix" the situation, but your summary should show that you were listening and applying empathy. Example summary: "Wow, really sounds like it was a hectic day, but great job with taking the lead on that project." This is called reflective listening and is an invaluable tool to use in an argument. It's a simple practice, but you'll be amazed at how quickly it can deepen your connection and significantly lessen conflict and misunderstandings.

By making "How Was Your Day?" a staple in your communication diet, you're not just exchanging information but fostering an environment of empathy, support, and mutual respect. It's about building a bridge between the every day and the exceptional in your relationship, ensuring they're shared, understood, and valued no matter how mundane or spectacular. So, why not give it a try? Turn this little game into a ritual, and watch as it transforms your way of communicating with each other.

Dream Sharing: Connecting on Future Aspirations

Think of your relationship as a canvas where both of you are artists, painting your hopes, dreams, and visions for the future. Sometimes, though, you might feel you're working on separate murals. Dream sharing is like setting up an easel and mixing your colors to create a masterpiece that reflects your aspirations. It's about turning to each other and saying, "Here's what I dream about doing, being, and achieving. What about you?" This isn't just chitchat; it's an invitation to build and dream together, to truly support each other's visions and weave them into a shared story of your future.

Let's break down why this matters. When you share your dreams with your partner, you're not just giving them a list of your bucket list items; you're opening up a part of your heart. It's showing them a side of you that's hopeful, maybe a bit scared, and deeply aspirational. This exchange nurtures a culture of support and encouragement. Imagine your partner wants to start their own business; discussing this dream can lead you to brainstorm ideas together, offer encouragement, and perhaps even help draft a business plan. It's more than support; it's active participation in each other's aspirations, reinforcing your bond. It tells your partner, "I believe in you, and I'm here with you on this journey."

Now, delving into dreams can make you feel quite vulnerable. It's like saying, "Here's what I truly desire," and waiting in that silent space, hoping for acceptance and encouragement. This act deepens your trust as you handle each other's hopes with care and respect. It's a delicate dance of give and take, where being vulnerable with your dreams and respecting your partner's dreams creates a foundation of trust that is both liberating and strengthening. This trust becomes the safety net that encourages taking risks and exploring potential, knowing you have a supportive partner cheering you on.

Moreover, discussing your dreams isn't just about the paths you wish to pursue; it's about finding where your paths converge. It's about discovering how your aspirations can align and support a shared vision for your future. Maybe you dream of buying a home in the mountains, and your partner dreams of writing a novel. How wonderful would it be to find a place that inspires your partner's writing while giving you the mountain retreat you long for? Aligning your dreams isn't about compromising so much: it is about enhancing your life's map that complements and strengthens each other. This alignment nurtures a partnership dynamic where both of you feel that your dreams matter and have a place in your shared life.

Keeping the conversation positive and forward-looking is vital. Dream sharing should be a source of inspiration and motivation, a way to toe the dialogue from the day-to tasks to exciting possibilities and shared adventures. It transforms routine conversations into dynamic discussions about options, encouraging both partners to think big and support each other's ambitions. This positivity is infectious; it brightens your mood and propels both of you towards making those dreams a reality. Instead of getting bogged down by the daily grind, you're lifted by the buoyancy of shared dreams and mutual support.

Incorporating dream sharing into your relationship routine can open new avenues of connection and understanding. It invites ongoing dialogue about what excites, scares, and drives you. It's a way to stay connected with who your partner is today and who they aspire to be tomorrow. And in doing so, you build a relationship that's not just about surviving together but thriving together.

The Appreciation Jar: Cultivating Gratitude

Imagine transforming your kitchen or living room into a little sanctuary of love and gratitude. Here's where the magic of the "Appreciation Jar" comes into play. This isn't just about saying 'thank you'—it's about creating a visible, tangible collection of why you cherish each other. Think of it as your treasure chest, where instead of gold and jewels, it's filled with notes that signify the wealth of your relationship. Each piece of paper holds words that affirm, uplift, and remind you why you're together, especially when life seems more like a stormy sea than smooth sailing.

Here's how it works: grab a jar (yes, any jar will do, though feel free to get crafty and decorate it to your heart's content) and a stack of note papers. Write down something you appreciate about your partner each day or as often as you can. Incorporate the kids too if you have kids and they are old enough to write gratitude notes. It could be a thank you for making lunch, I appreciate you always saying "have a good day," thank you for your patience in reading bedtime stories and being engaged and listening to our kids read or do math homework, or admiration for how they handled a stressful phone call. Fold these notes and drop them in the jar. This act, simple in its execution, is profound in its impact. It encourages you both to keep an eye out for the positives in each other, reinforcing a mindset of gratitude and appreciation. Before you know it, you're not just noticing the big gestures but also the myriad of small ways your partner intertwined beautifully in your life.

But the jar isn't just for show; it's interactive. Set a monthly or weekly date to sit together and read the notes. This can be an incredibly uplifting experience, especially during those inevitable moments when you might feel disconnected or taken for granted. Each note serves as a reminder of your partner's love and appreciation, acting like a mini emotional boost that can lift spirits and strengthen bonds. It's a way to relive those small, precious moments of connection and affection, reinforcing the emotional foundation of your relationship.

Incorporating this practice fosters a culture of acknowledgment and gratitude within your relationship. Regularly expressing appreciation not only enhances your emotional connection but also builds resilience. Relationships, like all things precious, require maintenance and care, and gratitude is a powerful tool in your relationship care kit. It helps to buffer against negativity bias—the tendency to pay more attention to the negative aspects of life. By filling your jar with positive affirmations, you create a reservoir of positive feelings that can help you navigate more challenging times with grace and compassion.

The beauty of the Appreciation Jar lies in its simplicity and the profound impact it can have on a relationship. It shifts the focus from what might be lacking to the abundance within your partnership. This shift enhances your day-to-day interactions and deepens your overall sense of collaboration and teamwork. You begin to see each other more fully, appreciate each other more deeply, and connect on a level that transcends life's everyday hustle and bustle.

As we wrap up this chapter on communication workouts, remember that each exercise we've explored is designed to strengthen the fabric of your relationship. From the daily debriefs of the "How Was Your Day?" game, the future-building discussions of "Dream Sharing," to the gratitude-infused interactions of the "Appreciation Jar," each activity is a step towards a more connected, resilient, and joyful partnership. These are tools not just to communicate better but to connect deeper, not just to coexist but to thrive together.

SEVENTEEN

Trust-Building Activities

L et's start with an activity that might sound a bit like a trust fall but with a twist—it involves a blindfold, a little adventure, and a great deal of faith in each other.

The Trust Walk: A Blindfolded Journey

Imagine this: one of you is blindfolded, completely unable to see your surroundings, while the other guides you through an unfamiliar path. It sounds like a scene from a reality TV show challenge, right? But really it's not just about getting from point A to point B. This exercise is a powerful metaphor for your relationship. The blindfolded partner must rely entirely on the other for guidance, placing immense trust in their partner's instructions. The guiding partner, on the other hand, must navigate the path with care and precision, ensuring their partner's safety and comfort throughout the journey.

This Trust Walk is a profound exercise in building trust through physical and emotional guidance. For the blindfolded, there's an undeniable vulnerability in not seeing where you're going and placing your complete trust in someone else's hands. It's about surrendering control—a challenge for many of us—and relying on your partner's directions. The guide's responsibility is immense; every instruction must be explicit and reassuring. "Take a small step to the left, there's a bump," or "Reach out your hand, there's a railing here"—these directions must be crisp and confident. It tests how well you communicate under pressure and how effectively you can support your partner when they're feeling vulnerable. Please don't take your partner to a ravine or a cliff. Pick a place where it is completely safe, and there isn't even the slightest possibility of danger.

Interactive Element: Reflection Section

After completing the Trust Walk, take a moment to reflect on the experience. Discuss how it felt to be the guide and the person being guided. Were there moments of anxiety or uncertainty? How did it feel to trust or to be trusted in such a tangible way? This reflection can open up discussions about trust in other areas of your relationship, making it a valuable tool for deeper understanding.

But the Trust Walk is more than just an exercise in guidance and communication; it's a unique shared experience that can significantly strengthen your bond. Stepping out of your comfort zones together and experiencing vulnerability and support creates a memorable moment you both will cherish. It's an adventure, a story you'll tell, laughing about that moment one of you almost walked into a bush or the relief you felt when your partner safely navigated you around a puddle.

Moreover, this activity enhances your reliance on each other. In relationships, much like in a Trust Walk, you'll sometimes feel vulnerable and unsure of the next step. You have a partner who can guide you, whom you can trust implicitly to lead the way when you feel lost. It solidifies the foundation of your relationship, ensuring that no matter how dark the path might seem, you've got each other to lean on, guide, and trust.

Engaging in the Trust Walk is a leap of faith, quite literally. It's about trusting your partner not just with your physical steps but also with your heart. While it might start with nervous laughter and tentative steps, it's a journey that leads to deeper trust, enhanced communication, and an unshakeable bond. So, grab that blindfold, find a safe space, and enter a trust-building experience that might transform how you walk through life together.

Sharing Histories: Understanding Each Other's Past

Have you ever sat down with your partner, maybe over a lazy Sunday brunch or during a long drive, and swapped stories from your "back in the day" vault? You know, those tales about your high school antics, the family vacations that never went as planned, or that first job where you were clueless but eager? Sharing these nuggets from your past isn't just a way to pass the time or get a few laughs—it's a treasure trove of insights that deepen your understanding of each other.

When you share stories of your past, you're not just recounting events; you're offering a window into the experiences that shaped you. This is about painting a picture of the younger you, the one who hadn't met your soulmate yet, who was still figuring out the world. Each story adds a stroke to the portrait of who you once were and, by extension, adds depth to who you are now. For instance, when you tell your partner about the time you stood up to a bully in school, you're not just sharing a victory moment but revealing a layer of your courage and justice. Or, when you recount the summers spent at your grandparents' farm, you offer a glimpse into your roots that sprouted your appreciation for tradition and family.

This sharing does more than entertain; it cultivates a garden of empathy. Understanding the challenges you each faced, whether it was struggling with studies, dealing with a strict parent, past childhood trauma, or overcoming a personal setback, naturally fosters a sense of empathy. It's one thing to know your partner as they are now, but understanding the journey they've been on, the hurdles they've overcome, and the triumphs they've celebrated adds a rich layer of compassion to your relationship. It helps you see why they might react strongly to criticism, value hard work so profoundly, or even have that quirky habit of triple-checking if the door is locked. It's about connecting the dots between past experiences and present behaviors, which can transform misunderstandings into moments of connection.

But here's the kicker: sharing these histories highlights your similarities and bridges your differences. It's like discovering who loved the same cartoon as kids or realizing how they dealt with similar situations differently. These revelations bring a sense of shared humanity and uniqueness to your relationship. You start to appreciate why your partner might approach things differently from you, which can be a gateway to celebrating your diversity instead of letting it drive you apart. It's about understanding that while your paths might have been different, they've brought you together to the same place.

Opening up about your personal history requires trust. It's about feeling safe enough to let your guard down and share aspects of your past that you may not reflect on often, even those parts that aren't wrapped in shiny paper. This vulnerability strengthens your trust because it's based on mutual respect and confidentiality. When you trust your partner with your stories, and they handle them with care, it reinforces your confidence in their love and support. This shared trust becomes a robust foundation on which your relationship can continue to build and flourish.

So next time you find yourselves curled up on the couch or taking a stroll down memory lane, remember that each shared story weaves a more colorful dynamic to your life together. It's not just about where you've been but how far you've come and how deeply you understand and appreciate each other. Each memory shared is a thread that ties your past to your present, making your bond unbreakable and uniquely yours.

Secret Swap: An Exercise in Vulnerability

Imagine this: you and your partner, maybe over a cozy dinner or during a quiet evening at home, decide to share something you've kept under wraps. It's not just chatter; it's about sharing a secret—a piece of yourself that you've kept shielded. This isn't about airing dirty laundry or unearthing skeletons from the closet just for the sake of it. It's about being vulnerable and showing trust by sharing a part of your little-known story. This is the essence of the Secret Swap exercise, an intimate exchange that can significantly enhance the emotional closeness between you and your partner.

The power of sharing a secret lies in the emotional openness it demands and cultivates. When you share something deeply personal, you're not just handing over information; you're handing over a piece of your heart. You're saying, "I trust you with this part of me that I don't usually share." This act can be incredibly affirming and can strengthen the bonds of intimacy. It's like letting someone in behind the walls you've carefully constructed, which can be terrifying and exhilarating. The vulnerability involved in this exchange is potent; it can transform the landscape of your relationship, making it richer and more connected.

But the magic of this exercise isn't just in the sharing; it's also in the reception. When your partner trusts you with their secret, it's a testament to the safety and strength of your bond. It's an unspoken affirmation that they see the relationship as a safe harbor for their profound truths. This safety is crucial because it lays the foundation for more open and honest communication. It encourages a culture where sharing and vulnerability are accepted and embraced. It's about creating an environment where both of you feel secure enough to share your fears, desires, and dreams, knowing they will be met with understanding and care, not judgment or dismissal.

Moreover, keeping each other's secrets is an essential exercise in trustworthiness. It's one thing to share a secret but another to hold it. You reinforce your trustworthiness and reliability by respecting the confidentiality of what your partner shares. It's a powerful affirmation that says, "Your inner world is safe with me." This aspect of the exercise can deepen trust very much, as each partner proves themselves a reliable confidant.

Additionally, this exercise provides invaluable insights into each other's inner worlds. Secrets often hold clues to fears, desires, and motivations that might not be visible. Understanding these deeper layers can lead to a better understanding of what drives and concerns your partner, which can be incredibly enlightening. It can explain certain behaviors or reactions that previously seemed puzzling, allowing you to empathize and support each other in more targeted and meaningful ways. For example, learning that your partner has always kept their artistic talents a secret because they were discouraged as a child can deepen your appreciation of their sensitivity and creativity. It might encourage you to support their creative pursuits, which brings you even closer to each other.

Engaging in a Secret Swap is like peeling back layers, revealing more of yourselves to each other. Doing so creates a world of shared confidence and mutual vulnerability. This world is not just beautiful but strong, capable of holding your relationship in a close, intimate embrace, even when challenges arise.

As we close this chapter on trust-building activities, remember that each exercise—from the Trust Walk and Sharing Histories to this Secret Swap—serves as a stepping stone towards a deeper, more resilient relationship. These activities are designed to weave trust, understanding, and support into the very fabric of your partnership, ensuring that as you move forward, you do so with a strong and secure foundation. Next, we'll explore rekindling romance, an essential aspect of navigating and nurturing any long-term commitment. Let's continue this adventure armed with the tools to strengthen our bonds and deepen our connections.

EIGHTEEN

Rekindling Romance

B e open to rebuilding and nurturing trust that the two of you rekindle and keep that flame lit. Sometimes, all it takes is stepping out of the usual routine and into something more exciting. Think of it as the relationship equivalent of ditching your favorite comfy pajamas for something more... intriguing. Let's dive into some date night ideas that can turn a regular evening into a treasure trove of new memories.

Date Night Ideas That Break the Routine

Imagine this: it's Thursday evening, you and your partner are sitting on the couch, scrolling through a never-ending sea of streaming options, but instead, you surprise your partner with a mystery box containing hints about a planned evening adventure. Suddenly, the energy changes, anticipation builds, and you're more engaged with each other than you've been in weeks.

Novel Experiences Enhance Connection

Breaking the monotony of your usual evening routine with unique date nights can reignite excitement and anticipation in your relationship. It's like turning a regular meal into a surprise tasting menu at a new restaurant—each dish brings a sense of discovery and delight. Planning something out of the ordinary, like a nighttime picnic under the stars or tickets to a quirky late-night show, provides a rush of novelty that can make you both feel more alive. And if you are a parent, arrange for family members or a babysitter to take care of kids for a date night. These date night experiences can be as simple as trying a new cuisine or as adventurous as a sponta- neous road trip to a nearby town. What matters is the break from routine, which shakes up your neural pathways and reignites those early relationship butterflies of excitement.

Promoting Quality Time Together

Setting aside specific times for these dates is crucial. It's about saying, "This time is ours, and nothing else matters right now." Whether it's a bi-weekly date night or a monthly day out, having that scheduled slot assures that you spend quality time together, focusing solely on each other. This commitment to shared time is vital in a world where everyone is perpetu- ally busy. It's a chance to slow down, catch up, and listen to each other without the constant interruptions of daily life. These moments can strengthen your emotional connection, reminding you both why you fell in love in the first place.

Encouraging Creativity and Playfulness

Coming up with innovative date ideas can also bring a sense of playfulness and creativity into your relationship. It's a chance to engage your imaginative sides together, brainstorming ideas that excite both of you. Maybe it's a themed dinner night where you both cook a dish from a different country or a scavenger hunt around your city with clues tied to your relationship milestones. I always get super excited and giddy when my husband says "I have a spot in mind, but I'm not going to tell you what it is. You will love it though." These creative ventures not only make for memorable dates but also show that you're willing to put in the effort to make your time together memorable. They say novelty is the spice of life, and in the case of relationships, it's the spark that keeps the romantic flame flickering.

Strengthening the Bond Through Shared Experiences

Lastly, these unique date nights are not just about having fun; they're about creating shared memories that add significant spice to your relationship. Each new experience is a story in the making that you'll both be part of. These stories become your private collection, bringing you closer and giving you a shared history and identity. When you look back at these moments, they become more than just dates; they are milestones of your journey together, each one reinforcing the bond you share.

Interactive Element: Date Night Idea Generator

To get the ball rolling, here's a fun exercise: the Date Night Idea Generator. Grab a piece of paper and jot down five activities you've thought about trying but haven't yet. Have your partner do the same. Then, cut these ideas into strips, fold them, and place them in a jar. Next time you plan a date night, pull out a strip at random—this will be your next adventure. This adds an element of surprise and ensures that both partners contribute to the pool of ideas, making the process engaging and exciting.

So, why settle for another night of the same old when you can put a dash of creativity and a sprinkle of adventure? Remember, the goal is not just to create fun dates but to foster a deeper connection, rekindle that romantic spark, and, most importantly, enjoy each other's company in new and heartwarming ways.

Love Letters: A Written Token of Affection

Remember the last time you encountered an old card or note from someone special? Remember that flutter, that warm rush of affection? Now, imagine giving that timeless gift to your partner. Yes, I'm talking about crafting a love letter, an old-school, pen-to-paper, heartfelt letter. It's not about poetic perfection or crafting the next literary classic. It's about putting your feelings down in ink, making them tangible, and creating something special and cherished.

Writing love letters or even poems is an art form that expresses affection and appreciation in one of the most personal ways possible. When you write a letter to your partner, you're taking the time to sit down and think about what they mean to you. It's about more than just saying "I love you"—explaining why and sharing what it is about them that lights up your world. Do their eyes crinkle when they laugh? Does their resilience inspire you? Write it all down. This isn't just another text or a quick "love you" as you rush out the door. It's your emotions, carefully considered and beautifully presented. It's your heart speaking directly to theirs, without the distractions or misunderstandings that can come with spoken words.

Moreover, these letters become keepsakes, a lasting reminder of your love and commitment. Unlike the fleeting conversations of daily life, a love letter remains. It can be tucked away in a drawer, only to be found on a difficult day when a little reassurance is needed, or it might be proudly displayed, a constant reminder of your bond. Each letter is a snapshot of your relationship at a particular moment, capturing your feelings and the stage of your relationship. As years pass, you and your partner can look back at these letters and see how you've grown together, how your love has evolved, and how you've navigated life's ups and downs as a team.

The act of writing these letters also encourages vulnerability. It's one thing to think loving thoughts, but another to write them down and hand them over, knowing they might be read repeatedly. This vulnerability is powerful; it deepens your emotional connection, reinforcing the trust and intimacy between you. It says, "I am open to you and trust you with my deepest feelings." This kind of openness can be incredibly affirming for your partner, showing them they are profoundly loved, valued, and understood.

Lastly, let's talk about the power of written words to express the complex, deep, and sometimes messy feelings we all experience but might struggle to express aloud. Maybe it is gratitude for being by your side during a brutal period, joy for the laughter and light they bring into your life, or even an apology for a past mistake. Writing gives you the chance to articulate these feelings clearly and thoughtfully. It lets you explain your emotions without interruption, providing a complete picture of your heart and mind. Plus, it will enable your partner to absorb your words fully without the immediate pressure to respond or the distractions of conversation.

So, grab a pen and a piece of paper and start writing. Tell your partner how much they mean to you, recount a cherished memory, or describe your hopes for the future together. Make it personal, heartfelt, and genuine. This letter could become a treasured token of your love, a testament to your relationship.

Creating a Bucket List Together

Imagine sitting down with your partner, a couple of mugs of your favorite beverage in hand, dreaming up all the wild, wonderful, and even wonderfully mundane things you'd like to do together in the coming years. This isn't just about crafting a list; it's about painting a canvas of your future adventures together. Creating a bucket list as a couple acts like a shared vision board—it's fun to dream up and incredibly bonding to plan and pursue these dreams together.

So, why is a bucket like setting GPS coordinates for a road trip? It gives you destination points you both agree on and are excited about. This shared list becomes your guide to building a rich life with experiences you both cherish.

Whether traveling to Iceland, snorkeling in Tahiti, or finally taking that cooking class to perfect your Filet Mignon-making skills, each item on your list represents a shared commitment to living a whole and adventurous life together. It's about saying, "Yes, let's make the most of our time," and ensuring that life doesn't just pass by in a blur of routine and responsibilities.

The process of creating this list can be pretty revealing. You'll discover more about what makes each other tick—maybe you never knew your partner dreamt of going on a road trip across the United States on the scenic route on old US 80. These revelations can open up new avenues of support and encouragement between you. For instance, if your partner reveals a secret desire to learn painting, you might surprise them with brushes and paints. These supportive acts reinforce your bond, showing that you're not just listening but actively encouraging each other's dreams and personal growth.

Encourages Adventure and Growth

Pursuing these bucket list adventures can lead to significant growth in your relationship. Each new experience is a mini-adventure that takes you out of your comfort zone and encourages you to rely on each other differently. Maybe it's navigating a foreign city where neither of you speaks the language, or it's supporting each other through the challenges of learning a new skill. These experiences can strengthen your partnership as you tackle obstacles and celebrate successes together. They remind you that you're not just lovers or roommates but teammates on this exciting life journey.

Moreover, these adventures keep the relationship fresh and dynamic. It's easy to fall into a routine where predictability becomes the norm, and while stability is comforting, too much of it can dampen the vibrant energy that keeps a relationship exciting. By injecting new experiences into your lives, you maintain that spark of excitement and curiosity that brought you together in the first place.

Moreover, working together to achieve these bucket list goals can enhance your teamwork skills. It requires planning, communication, compromise, and sometimes a great deal of patience. These qualities strengthen a relationship, making it more resilient and deeply connected. Each checkmark on your bucket list is a testament to your ability to work together, support each other's dreams, and build a life that's rich with shared aspirations.

Providing a Roadmap for Future Experiences

Finally, your bucket list serves as a roadmap for your relationship. It helps you align your long-term goals and ensures you're both moving in the same direction. It's a living document that can evolve as you do, adapting to new dreams, circumstances, and ideas. This flexibility is critical to keeping the list relevant and exciting. Maybe what matters in your twenties shifts as you enter your forties, fifties, sixties. That's okay! The list is meant to reflect your growth as individuals and as a couple, ensuring that no matter what stage of life you're in, you have goals to look forward to together.

As we wrap up this exploration of rekindling romance through dates, letters, and bucket lists, remember that each step you take towards strengthening your bond is a step towards a more prosperous, more fulfilling partnership.

These efforts make the relationship more vibrant, resilient, and deeply connected. Let these shared experiences, dreams, and adventures be the chapters of your love story that you write together, each page filled with laughter, love, and the joy of shared discovery. As we turn the page to the next chapter, we'll delve into exploring ways to navigate mental health in relationships.

NINETEEN

Addressing Mental Health in Relationships

I magine you're trying to solve a jigsaw puzzle, but a few pieces seem to be hiding under the couch, elusive and just out of reach. That's a bit like trying to understand mental health in a relationship, especially when signs of anxiety or depression begin to influence the dynamic. It's not always clear what's part of the usual ebb and flow of someone's mood and what signals something more significant. Recognizing these signs early on can be like finding those puzzle pieces – suddenly, everything makes more sense, and you can see the picture more clearly.

Recognizing Signs of Anxiety and Depression

When it comes to mental health, being a proactive partner can sometimes mean the difference between a problem that's manageable and one that grows silently more complex. Recognizing the signs of anxiety and depression in your partner isn't about becoming an overnight psychiatrist.

Instead, it's about tuning into changes affecting the person you love. You know your partner, their quirks, and their ups and downs. But when you start to notice that their lows are getting more profound and the downs are sticking around a bit too long, it might be time to consider that what you're seeing could be signs pointing to anxiety or depression.

Leave that to the professionals; this isn't about diagnosing but noticing. Is your partner sleeping more or less than usual? Have they lost interest in activities they used to love? Maybe they're more irritable, or their anxiety over daily tasks seems amplified. These changes can be subtle or stark, but they're often persistent. It's as if they've been wearing sunglasses indoors—day in and day out—and you can't help but notice that something just doesn't seem right.

Addressing these observations can be tricky. You want to be supportive without seeming invasive. It's about offering a hand to hold rather than trying to pull them out of whatever they're experiencing by force. Encouraging professional help is a delicate dance. It involves expressing your concerns without making assumptions about their feelings. You might say, "I've noticed you've been feeling down lately, and I think it could help to talk to someone about it who could objectively offer emotional support. What do you think?" It's supportive, non-judgmental, and leaves the ball in their court, respecting their autonomy and promoting a sense of agency in their healing process.

Interactive Element: Reflective Journaling Prompt

Why not take a moment to reflect on this? Consider journaling about the changes you've noticed. Writing them down can help you process what you're observing and prepare you for a conversation with your partner. It's not about keeping score but about keeping track in a constructive and caring way.

The impact of untreated mental health issues like anxiety and depression on a relationship can be devastating. Communication might begin to fray as misunderstandings become more frequent. Intimacy might wane as one partner struggles with feelings they might not fully understand. The relationship might feel under a constant cloud cover, where moments of joy seem fleeting. Addressing these issues head-on, with compassion and understanding, can feel like bringing an umbrella into the rain—not necessarily stopping the storm but offering a shared protection that helps you move forward together.

Navigating mental health challenges in a relationship is about patience, understanding, and a lot of communication. It's about recognizing that these challenges are not the entirety of your partner or your relationship but are hurdles you can overcome together. It's about adjusting expectations and finding new ways to support each other through life's ups and downs. Most importantly, it's about ensuring that love, compassion, and empathy are part of every conversation, every gesture, and every approach to dealing with these genuine challenges.

Supporting a Partner with Mental Health Challenges

When your partner is navigating the rough waters of mental health challenges, think of yourself as the supportive light-house, offering a steady light to guide them through. Important note: being that beacon doesn't mean you have all the answers or can calm the storm. It means understanding the storm, knowing when to offer shelter, and when to shine a light on their path simply. Educating yourself about your partner's struggles is the first step in this supportive journey. It's not about becoming an expert overnight but about understanding the nuances of their experiences. Whether it's anxiety, depression, or any other mental health condition, knowing the symptoms, triggers, and potential treatments can make a significant difference. It empowers you to anticipate rough seas, recognize when they might need a life jacket, and provide it without them having to ask for it every time.

Support, however, has another side to it—boundaries. It might seem counterintuitive, but setting boundaries is essential in caring for yourself and your partner. Think of it like this: who will guide the ship if you're both lost in the storm? Setting boundaries helps prevent burnout on your end and fosters a healthier dynamic in your relationship. It's about knowing how much support you can give without losing yourself. This could mean agreeing on specific times to talk through feelings when you're both available and can give the conversation the attention it deserves. It might involve recognizing when you're out of your depth and suggesting a professional's help instead. These boundaries aren't walls keeping you apart; they're guardrails keeping you both safe on your journey together.

Now, let's talk communication— Effective communication in the context of mental health requires openness, patience, and a lot of listening. Start conversations with open-ended questions encouraging your partner to express themselves fully, like "What can I do to support you right now?" rather than "Do you want to talk about it?" This approach opens up a space for them to share their needs and feelings without feeling pressured. It's also crucial to respond with empathy and validation, acknowledging their feelings without immediately trying to fix them. This can be as simple as saying, "That sounds tough. I'm here for you," rather than immediately jumping in with solutions or advice.

Lastly, pay attention to the power of couples therapy. It's like having a skilled navigator join you on your journey, helping to map out the uncharted waters of mental health within your relationship. Couples therapy provides a safe space to explore these issues with a professional who can guide you in understanding each other's perspectives, improving communication, and strengthening your relationship. It's not about pointing fingers but tackling the challenges together as a team. Whether learning new coping strategies, understanding each other's emotional languages, or simply having a mediator to help navigate difficult conversations, couples therapy can be an invaluable resource in your relationship toolkit.

Navigating mental health challenges in a relationship is no small feat. It requires compassion, patience, and a willingness to learn and grow together. But with the right tools and a commitment to support each other, you can weather the storm and come out stronger on the other side. Remember, it's not about fixing everything—it's about understanding, supporting, and walking together, hand in hand, through whatever comes your way.

Self-Care: Keeping Your Own Cup Full

Imagine you're on a long-haul flight that stretches through the night and spills into the next day. You've heard it a million times: "In an emergency, secure your oxygen mask before helping others." It's a principle that holds not just in the air but on the ground, especially when you're playing a supportive role in a relationship where mental health challenges are present. It's essential to keep your cup full or, let's say, your oxygen mask firmly in place. This is not about being selfish; it's about maintaining your mental and emotional well-being so you can be present and supportive without crashing yourself.

Let's talk about what self-care means. Self-care is about more than just bubble baths and spa days. It's about taking tangible steps to maintain your health and happiness, which, in turn, allows you to be the rock your partner might need. For instance, it might mean setting aside time for a hobby that lights you up, whether it is going to your favorite Japanese restaurant and ordering sushi, or going hiking, or strumming the guitar. It's these activities that refill your energy reserves and keep you grounded. Remember to review my previous guidebook, "5 Categories of Self Care: The Ultimate Guide to Finding Self Love and Happiness."

Identifying personal needs and boundaries is another critical aspect of self-care. Here's where communication with yourself becomes as important as communication with your partner. Take time to check in with yourself regularly: How are you feeling? What do you need more or less of? This is part of Spiritual Self Care. Recognizing and honoring these needs isn't a luxury; it's a necessity. It helps prevent resentment from seeping into your relationship and keeps you from burning out.

Regarding practical self-care activities, think about how you can tie in healthy new habits in day to day routines. It might be as simple as ensuring enough sleep, managing a healthy diet, or maintaining a regular exercise routine. Mindfulness practices like meditation or yoga may resonate with you, helping you stay centered and calm. Or maybe it's about carving out time for social activities that don't involve your partner, allowing you to recharge with friends or family? These activities aren't just checkboxes on a wellness to-do list; they're lifelines that keep you afloat, ensuring you have the energy and emotional space to handle the ups and downs of supporting a partner through mental health challenges.

Finally, don't underestimate the power of leveraging your support networks. It's lovely to be a pillar of support for your partner, but even pillars need a solid foundation. This is part of your Social Self Care. Your friends, family, or community support groups can play this role. They can offer a listening ear, a different perspective, or an escape when things get heavy. These networks remind you that you're not alone, providing a safety net of emotional and practical support. Whether it's a friend who makes you laugh, a family member who offers wise advice, or a support group where you can share your experiences, these connections are invaluable. They strengthen your resilience and enrich your life, making you a more balanced and joyful person, which benefits both you and your partner.

Navigating a relationship where mental health plays a significant role can sometimes feel very daunting and isolating. Caring for your partner and not losing sight of your needs is a delicate balance. By focusing on self-care, you ensure that you're a supportive partner and a healthy, happy individual. This isn't just beneficial for you; it's essential for the longevity and health of your relationship.

As we wrap up our discussion on mental health in relationships, remember the importance of recognizing signs, providing support, and prioritizing self-care. These elements are crucial not only for your partner's health but also for your relationship's vitality. Next, we will explore how to navigate the complex emotions and practicalities when dealing with infidelity, ensuring that our journey through relationship resilience continues with compassion and understanding.

TWENTY

Navigating Infidelity and Trust Rebuilding

Infidelity can feel like you were in a horrific car crash, and your entire life feels like it has been crumpled into bits of the car that has been destroyed by the crash. It is a sudden, startling revelation that the picture of your relationship you held isn't entirely accurate. It's confusing, and heart-wrenching, and you're left with pieces that don't seem to fit anymore. But understanding why the infidelity happened is the first step towards picking up those pieces and seeing if your car can be reassembled into something new, something sturdier.

Understanding Why Infidelity Happens

Infidelity Has Multifaceted Causes

Infidelity doesn't come from nowhere, even though it might feel like a bolt out of the blue. It's often the result of a tangled web of unmet needs, emotional disconnections, and sometimes the allure of external temptations. Think of your relationship as a garden. If you stop tending to it, stop watering it, or if you only pay attention to a tiny corner of it, the rest of the garden starts wilting, and weeds begin to grow. Emotional disconnection occurs when partners no longer share their inner worlds or when "How was your day?" becomes a reflex rather than a genuine question.

This disconnection can create a void. This is where unmet needs come into play. If someone feels neglected and unappreciated, and if their physical needs are unmet, they might be more susceptible to external temptations. It's not about excusing the behavior but rather understanding the environment in which it took root. It's about recognizing that plants —like relationships—need consistent nurturing to stay healthy.

The Role of Communication in Understanding Infidelity

The saying "communication is key" might be cliché, but it's as accurate as ever when unraveling the threads of infidelity. Open, honest communication can sometimes unearth painful truths but also pave the way for healing. It's like setting a broken bone: painful but necessary for proper healing. Discussing the reasons behind infidelity isn't about assigning blame. It's about gaining clarity. Why did it happen? What was missing in the relationship? How can we ensure it doesn't happen again? These are tough questions, requiring a level of honesty that can be brutal. But this brutal honesty can potentially lead to deeper understanding and stronger bonds.

Different Forms of Infidelity

Infidelity isn't just physical. It's essential to recognize that emotional and digital infidelities exist and can be just as damaging, if not more so. Emotional infidelity might involve forming a deep, intimate connection with someone else, one that usurps the emotional place of a partner. Digital infidelity, on the other hand, might involve secret, intimate conversations online or through texts. Each type affects relationships differently but shares a common thread: the breach of trust.

The Impact of Societal and Personal Values

Our societal and personal values deeply influence our reactions to infidelity. What one person considers a forgivable lapse, another might view as an unforgivable betrayal. Understanding these values can help contextualize the feelings around infidelity. Instead of asking, "How could they do this to me?" ask, "What are our definitions of infidelity? What does it mean to us?" This understanding doesn't excuse the hurt caused but can deepen the understanding of why the betrayal feels so profound.

Interactive Element: Reflection Section

Consider reflecting on what trust means to you. How do you define infidelity? Is it physical, emotional, digital, or all of the above? How do these definitions align with your partner's? Understanding these facets can provide a more transparent framework as you navigate the complexities of rebuilding trust.

Navigating the aftermath of infidelity is undeniably painful. It's a process that involves deconstructing and reconstructing not just the relationship but often your self-concept. But with understanding, patience, and hard work, it's possible to piece together a new, more resilient picture of your relationship. Whether this picture resembles the old one or if it becomes something entirely new depends on the paths you choose to take from here.

The Road to Reconciliation: Steps to Rebuild Trust

When mending the bridge of trust after it's been torched by infidelity, think of it not as a quick patch-up job but as a careful architectural rebuild. It's important to understand that trust, once broken, doesn't snap back like a stretched rubber band. It's more akin to nurturing a bruised plant back to health—it needs time, the right conditions, and a heap of patience from both the gardener and the plant. Rebuilding trust is a journey of rediscovery and renewal that both partners must commit to, understanding that the landscape of your relationship might forever hold the scars of past hurts. Still, like seasoned wood, it could be more vital for them.

Firstly, let's talk about patience and commitment. Rebuilding trust isn't a linear process, and there will be days when it feels like you're making incredible progress and others where the ghosts of past mistakes might cloud your sunny skies. The key here is commitment. Both partners need to be in it for the long haul. This means consistent actions that build trust over time, regular check-ins on feelings and thoughts, and a mutual understanding that setbacks aren't roadblocks but natural parts of the healing process. It's like following a recipe; you need to keep at it, even if it doesn't turn out perfect every time, because eventually, you'll get the hang of it and start to taste as it should.

Let's delve into forgiveness, a hefty but crucial ingredient in the trust rebuild. Forgiveness in the context of infidelity doesn't mean excusing the act or forgetting it happened. Refer back to Forgiveness Therapy chapter 3 and the four phases. Forgiveness is about releasing the burden of pain so you're not carrying it around like a backpack full of bricks. It's about saying, "I acknowledge what happened; it hurt me deeply, but I choose not to let it control my emotions and our future." This takes work, and it takes time. It's a daily choice; some days will be more complex than others. It involves understanding the underlying issues that led to the betrayal and addressing them not as justifications but as part of under-standing the whole picture. Forgiveness might mean more to the one who was hurt, as it allows them to find peace and gradually open up to trust again.

Switching gears to communication, after infidelity, the old communication patterns won't cut it. New, healthier ways to share feelings, fears, and needs are needed. This new commu-nication pattern involves more transparency and less assump-tion. It's about saying what you mean clearly and listening deeply when your partner speaks. Think of it as upgrading your old radio to a high-definition sound system; suddenly, you're picking up on nuances you never noticed before. This might involve scheduled talks where you check in on each other's feelings and the state of your relationship, or it might involve learning to argue better—focusing on the issue instead of attacking each other's characters.

Lastly, professional guidance is not just a nice-to-have but often a must-have in navigating the murky waters post-infidelity. A therapist or counselor can act like a lighthouse, offering guidance and illuminating blind spots in your relationship that you might not know. They provide a safe space to explore painful feelings, understand complex emotions, and learn practical tools to rebuild trust. They can help you navigate your feelings and ensure your path toward reconciliation is healthy and productive. Think of them as the guide on your hiking trip; while you do the walking, they ensure you don't stray from the path or fall down a ravine.

Rebuilding trust after infidelity is tough. There's no sugar-coating it. But with patience, a commitment to process and change, a willingness to forgive, and a commitment to better communication, along with some professional help, it's possible to patch up the trust landscape of your relationship. It might never look the same, but sometimes, what you rebuild can become more robust and beautiful in its resilience and complexity.

TWENTY-ONE

Preventing Future Betrayals: Strengthening Your Bond

I magine your relationship as a cozy, well-built cabin in the woods. It's sturdy, filled with warm memories, and a place of refuge. However, like any suitable structure, it requires maintenance to keep it secure from the storms it might face. This analogy brings us to the importance of being proactive in your relationship to prevent future betrayals. Being proactive isn't about suspecting your partner or fearing another betrayal; it's about nurturing your relationship to make it so robust that the thought of infidelity becomes more distant.

A vital part of this proactive approach involves understanding and actively meeting each other's emotional and physical needs. It's easy to slip into a routine where these needs might be overlooked or assumed to be satisfied. However, just like you wouldn't think a plant needs no water just because it's not wilting, don't assume your partner's needs are met just because they haven't voiced discontent. Open a dialogue about what you both desire and need from the relationship, whether it's more quality time together, deeper communication, or a more satisfying physical connection. Sometimes, it's about asking simple questions like, "What can I do for you that I haven't done in a while?" or "How can I make you feel more loved?" These questions can open up discussions that preempt feelings of neglect or emotional disconnect that might lead to seeking fulfillment elsewhere.

Setting boundaries with external parties is also crucial. This isn't about cutting ties with friends or colleagues but rather about establishing clear limits that protect the integrity of your relationship. For instance, deciding not to discuss your personal relationship details with coworkers or agreeing that spending time alone with certain friends who pose a temptation is off-limits. Think of these boundaries as not restrictions but protective guidelines that help keep your relationship healthy. It's like knowing you shouldn't bring sand to the beach—not because it's wrong, but because it doesn't contribute positively to your place.

Regular relationship check-ins are another vital component. These check-ins can be like your relationship's State of the Union address. It's a dedicated time to discuss what's working well and what might need more attention without the distractions of daily life. These discussions can cover everything from emotional fulfillment to your sex life, ensuring that no concern is too small to be acknowledged. It's about creating a safe space for both partners to express their feelings and needs openly. Consider these check-ins as tune-ups for your relationship, which are essential for keeping it running smoothly and addressing any minor issues before they become significant problems.

Reflective Journaling Prompt

Take time to jot down what proactive steps you could take this month to strengthen your relationship. Consider areas like emotional intimacy, physical connection, boundary setting, and communication. How can you turn these ideas into actions that fortify your bond against potential storms?

By taking these proactive steps, ycu safeguard your relationship against future betrayals and enrich the quality of your connection, making it more fulfilling and resilient. It's about building a love that's not just weathering storms but thriving in clear skies.

As we wrap up this exploration of trust and infidelity, remember that every step you take towards strengthening your relationship is a brick in the fortress of your love. These proactive measures aren't just safeguards against pain; they affirm your love and respect for each other. As we close this chapter, we understand that while the road to recovery from betrayal is challenging, the journey to a stronger, more connected partnership is rich with opportunities for growth and deepening love. Let's continue to build, protect, and cherish our bonds with the promise of a brighter, more secure future together.

Conclusion

Well, here we are at the end of our journey together through the maze of couples therapy. From the first pages, where we tackled the essence of communication, to exploring the depths of trust and vulnerability and even figuring out how to handle the double-edged sword of technology in relationships, we've covered a lot of ground.

Let's take a moment to recap the treasures we've unearthed. We began by establishing a solid foundation with open communication, ensuring both partners feel heard and valued. Remember the importance of those 'I' statements? They weren't just fancy jargon but tools to express yourself without putting your partner on the defensive. We also discussed the importance of self care and independent happiness and removing self from toxic relationships that are not elevating your happiness. We ventured into the realms of vulnerability, highlighting how letting your guard down is a badge of bravery that invites deeper intimacy.

We didn't stop there. We rolled up our sleeves, got our hands dirty with proactive conflict resolution strategies, and reinforced the significance of personal growth within your relationship. Each chapter brought us exercises and activities designed not just to be read but to be lived. These aren't just pages to flip through; they're steps to walk through your daily life, enriching your relationship one day at a time.

Reflecting on our discussion about technology, it's clear that while digital tools have the power to connect, they also require us to navigate a new set of challenges. Finding that sweet spot where technology supports rather than sabotages your connection is critical. Setting boundaries around social media use or scheduling a digital date night is about making technology work for you.

Building a fulfilling relationship isn't a one-and-done deal—it's an ongoing adventure. It's about committing to grow, communicate, and love through the easy breezes and stormy weather. I encourage you to keep using the tools and insights we've explored to face challenges as they come not with fear but with anticipation of the growth they will bring.

And remember, it's okay to ask for directions on this journey. Seeking help from a therapist or counselor isn't a defeat; it's a strategic move towards a healthier, more substantial relationship. It's about playing to win together.

If this book has been a helpful companion on your journey, I'd love for you to share your story. Whether it's a quiet recommendation to a friend or a shout from the digital rooftops on Amazon reviews, let's spread the word that relationships can be beautifully transformative with the right tools and a dash of courage.

As we close this chapter (pun intended), I leave you with a heart full of hope. May this book light your way as you navigate the path of your relationship? Here's to believing in the incredible power of love and commitment to overcome any obstacle. Keep loving, keep fighting, and most importantly, keep growing together.

With all my heart and a little extra for the road, Katherine Ibarra

References

5 Categories of Self Care: The Ultimate Guide to Finding Self Love and Happiness: Ibarra, Katherine: 9798325336379: Amazon.com: Books. (n.d.). https://a.co/d/gl0UCk7

PsyD, J. S. (2024, July 25). *Forgiveness Therapy: 6+ techniques to help clients Forgive.* PositivePsychology.com. https://positivepsychology.com/forgiveness-in-therapy/

Nonverbal Communication and Body Language https://www.helpguide.org/articles/relationships-communication/nonverbal-communication.htm

How to Practice Active Listening: 16 Examples & Techniques https://positivepsychology.com/active-listening-techniques/

Nine Steps to a Successful Difficult Conversation With Your ... https://helenebrenner.com/nine-steps-for-a-successful-difficult-conversation/

The Body Language of Couples in Love https://www.psychologytoday.com/us/blog/cutting-edge-leadership/202211/the-body-language-couples-in-love

The Importance of Vulnerability in Healthy Relationships https://www.psychologytoday.com/us/blog/happy-healthy-relationships/202203/the-importance-vulnerability-in-healthy-relationships

How to Deal with Betrayal: 8 Tips - Psych Central https://psychcentral.com/health/dealing-with-betrayal

Dating and Relationships in the Digital Age https://www.pewresearch.org/internet/2020/05/08/dating-and-relationships-in-the-digital-age/

How to speak with your partner about digital boundaries https://www.joinonelove.org/learn/how-to-speak-with-your-partner-about-digital-boundaries/

7 Ways to Improve Communication in Relationships https://positivepsychology.com/communication-in-relationships/

3 WAYS THAT UNRESOLVED CONFLICT CAN ... https://www.bocaratoncouplestherapy.com/3-ways-that-unresolved-conflict-can-negatively-influence-your-couples-relationship/

How to Make Repair Attempts So Your Partner Feels Loved https://www.gottman.com/blog/make-repair-attempts-partner-feels-loved/

Expectations & Negotiations: Couples Who Compromise, Thrive https://centerstone.org/our-resources/health-wellness/expectations-negotiations-couples-who-compromise-thrive/

Daily Rituals of Connection - The Gottman Institute https://www.gottman.com/blog/3-daily-rituals-that-stop-spouses-from-taking-each-other-for-granted/

Vulnerability in Relationships: Tips From a Marriage Counselor https://iditsharoni.com/the-power-of-vulnerability-in-relationships-insights-from-a-marriage-counselor/

Direct Effects of Marital Empathy, Body Image, and Perceived ... https://www.ncbi.nlm.nih.gov/pmc/articles/PMC10896763/#:

How to Conquer these 4 Damaging Communication Barriers https://ftajax.com/4-damaging-communication-barriers/

How To Feel Comfortable Expressing Sexual Desires With ... https://www.gottman.com/blog/how-to-feel-comfortable-expressing-sexual-desires-with-your-partner/

6 Ways How Shame Can Undermine Intimacy https://www.psychologytoday.com/us/blog/overcoming-destructive-anger/202207/6-ways-how-shame-can-undermine-intimacy

9 Powerful Intimacy Exercises to Feel More Connected https://practicalintimacy.com/marriage-intimacy-exercises-for-couples/

The Role of Partner Novelty in Sexual Functioning: A Review. https://www.researchgate.net/publication/265649086_The_Role_of_Partner_Novelty_in_Sexual_Functioning_A_Review

Why Is Personal Growth So Important In Long-Term ... https://www.linkedin.com/pulse/why-personal-growth-so-important-long-term-louis-morris

9 Activities for Couples to Develop a Healthy and Happy Relationship https://www.bookofus.com/blog/2020/03/10/%E2%80%8B9-activities-for-couples-to-develop-a-healthy-and-happy-relationship/

4 Ways to Keep Your Identity in a Relationship - Psych Central https://psychcentral.com/health/why-men-give-up-their-identity-in-a-relationship#:

Autonomy–connection tensions, stress, and attachment https://www.ncbi.nlm.nih.gov/pmc/articles/PMC8881097/

A Guide to Financial Planning for Couples https://www.monarchmoney.com/blog/financial-planning-for-couples

Boundaries, In-Laws, and Extended Families: Creating ... https://www.decaroparentcoaching.com/blog/boundaries-in-laws-and-extended-families-creating-relationships-that-work-for-everybody/

How to Protect Your Relationship from Work Stress https://greatergood.berkeley.edu/article/item/how_to_protect_your_relationship_from_work_stress

Your Marriage Or Your Job? How To Balance Your Career ... https://www.forbes.com/sites/erikaboissiere/2019/10/24/your-marriage-or-your-job-how-to-balance-your-career-and-your-relationship/

The Unspoken Struggles of Moving for Your Partner's Job https://www.linkedin. com/pulse/balancing-love-career-unspoken-struggles-moving-your-job-pederson-flbic

Couple's Relationship during the Transition to Parenthood ... https://www.ncbi. nlm.nih.gov/pmc/articles/PMC9819747/

How to Be a Supportive Partner During a Career Change https://www.success. com/how-to-support-a-partner-in-career-change/

How to Keep the Romantic Spark Alive After Baby - The Bump https://www. thebump.com/a/revving-up-your-sex-life-after-baby

8 Communication Exercises in Long-Distance Relationships https://blog.zencare. co/long-distance-relationship-communication/

Blended Family and Step-Parenting Tips https://www.helpguide.org/articles/ parenting-family/step-parenting-blended-families.htm

8 Ways to Bridge the Age Gap in Your Relationship - Brides https://www.brides. com/handle-age-differences-in-relationships-2303199

Enhancing relationships through technology: directions in ... https://www.ncbi. nlm.nih.gov/pmc/articles/PMC7366940/

6 Therapist-Approved Communication Exercises For Couples https://www.sdrela tionshipplace.com/communication-exercises-for-couples/

Giving Thanks: How Gratitude Strengthens Relationships https://www.psycholo gytoday.com/us/blog/evidence-based-living/202311/giving-thanks-how-gratitude-strengthens-relationships

Why Vulnerability in Relationships Is So Important https://www.verywellmind. com/why-vulnerability-in-relationships-is-so-important-5193728

Rituals Strengthen Couples. Here's Why They're Good for ... https://hbswk.hbs. edu/item/rituals-strengthen-couples-here-s-why-they-re-good-for-busi ness-too

12 Proven Trust-Building Exercises to Repair ... https://riveroakspsychology. com/12-proven-trust-building-exercises-to-repair-relationships-of-all-types/

How to Build Trust in a Relationship, According to a Therapist https://www.very wellmind.com/how-to-build-trust-in-a-relationship-5207611

17 Communication Exercises for Couples Therapy https://www.talkspace.com/ blog/communication-exercises-for-couples-therapy/

The Importance of Vulnerability in Healthy Relationships https://www.psycholo gytoday.com/us/blog/happy-healthy-relationships/202203/the-impor tance-vulnerability-in-healthy-relationships

Couples' Shared Participation in Novel and Arousing ... https://www.research gate.net/profile/Elaine-Aron/publication/12609069_Couples% 27_shared_participation_in_novel_and_arousing_activities_and_experi enced_relationship_quality/links/5577bd0f08aeacff20004ef3/Couples-shared-participation-in-novel-and-arousing-activities-and-experienced-relationship-quality.pdf

17 Reasons Why Quality Time in a Relationship Is Important https://www.marriage.com/advice/relationship/relationships-need-quality-time/

Letter Writing as a Couples Activity to Increase Intimacy https://www.goodtherapy.org/blog/letter-writing-as-couples-activity-to-increase-intimacy-0906164/

The Ritual of Setting Goals Together https://www.psychologytoday.com/us/blog/happy-healthy-relationships/202401/the-ritual-of-setting-goals-together

Depression (major depressive disorder) - Symptoms and ... https://www.mayoclinic.org/diseases-conditions/depression/symptoms-causes/syc-20356007

Setting Healthy Boundaries in Relationships https://www.helpguide.org/articles/relationships-communication/setting-healthy-boundaries-in-relationships.htm

Strengthening Mental Health in Couples ... https://mindfullyhealing.com/the-power-of-communication-strengthening-mental-health-in-couples/

Benefits of Couples Counseling and How It Works https://www.verywellhealth.com/couples-counseling-5205837

Why Do People in Relationships Cheat? https://www.scientificamerican.com/article/why-do-people-in-relationships-cheat/

Communication After Infidelity is Hard: Here Are 5 Tips to Improve It https://themarriagerestorationproject.com/communication-after-infidelity-is-hard-here-are-5-tips-to-improve-it/

How to Build Trust with Your Partner After Infidelity https://www.gottman.com/blog/how-to-build-trust-with-your-partner-after-infidelity/

Setting and Respecting Healthy Boundaries in Marriage https://www.thecouplescenter.org/setting-and-respecting-healthy-boundaries-in-marriage/

Dating and Relationships in the Digital Age https://www.pewresearch.org/internet/2020/05/08/dating-and-relationships-in-the-digital-age/

How to speak with your partner about digital boundaries https://www.joinonelove.org/learn/how-to-speak-with-your-partner-about-digital-boundaries/

The Unique Advantages Of Online Couples Counseling https://www.betterhelp.com/advice/relations/benefits-of-online-couple-counseling/

7 Apps for Couples That Will Help Improve Your Relationship https://thebudgetsavvybride.com/apps-for-couples-improve-relationship/